THE ART OF POETRY

Seven Lectures

1920—1922

THE ART OF POETRY
Seven Lectures
1920—1922

BY

WILLIAM PATON KER

Fellow of All Souls College
Professor of Poetry

Essay Index Reprint Series

BOOKS FOR LIBRARIES PRESS, INC.
FREEPORT, NEW YORK

First Published 1923
Reprinted 1967

LIBRARY OF CONGRESS CATALOG CARD NUMBER: 67-26752

PN
1136
K4
1967

PRINTED IN THE UNITED STATES OF AMERICA

TO

ARTHUR LIONEL SMITH

MASTER OF BALLIOL

CONTENTS

PAGE

2005

THE ART OF POETRY

I WISH I could say how deeply I feel what I owe to the generous and sanguine friends who have elected me to this most honourable Chair. It would be less difficult to find words for the danger of the task; this is the Siege Perilous. But I will not attempt to say in full what I think and feel most sincerely with regard to the honour you have done me; as for the hazards of the place, they must be manifest to every one who has spent any time at all in thinking of the Art of Poetry. But you will allow me to say as much as this, that I find the greatest encouragement and the best auspices in those who have held this Chair before me; and I ask leave in this place to thank Mr. Bradley, Mr. Mackail, and the President of Magdalen for their good wishes.

DRUMMOND of Hawthornden, writing his sentiments about a new fashion in poetry which displeased him, begins with some old-fashioned sentences which may afford a text here; in a letter addressed ' to his much-honoured friend M. A. J., Physician to the King '. His friend is the poet Arthur Johnston, ' who holds among the Latin poets of Scotland the next place to

the elegant Buchanan'. Drummond is writing
to a man of the highest principles, as follows :

'It is more praiseworthy in noble and excellent
things to know something, though little, than in mean
and ignoble matters to have a perfect knowledge.
Amongst all those rare ornaments of the mind of Man
Poesie hath had a most eminent place and been in
high esteem, not only at one time, and in one climate,
but during all times and through those parts of the
world where any ray of humanity and civility hath
shined. So that she hath not unworthily deserved the
name of the Mistress of human life, the height of
eloquence, the quintessence of knowledge, the loud
trumpet of Fame, the language of the Gods. There
is not anything endureth longer : Homer's Troy hath
outlived many Republics, and both the Roman and
Grecian Monarchies ; she subsisteth by herself, and
after one demeanour and continuance her beauty
appeareth to all ages. In vain have some men of
late (transformers of everything) consulted upon her
reformation, and endeavoured to abstract her to metaphysical ideas and scholastical quiddities, denuding her
of her own habits, and those ornaments with which
she hath amused the world some thousand years.
Poesie is not a thing that is in the finding and search,
or which may be otherwise found out, being already
condescended upon by all nations, and as it were
established *iure gentium* amongst Greeks, Romans,
Italians, French, Spaniards. Neither do I think that
a good piece of *Poesie* which Homer, Virgil, Ovid,
Petrarch, Bartas, Ronsard, Boscan, Garcilasso (if they

were alive and had that language) could not understand, and reach the sense of the writer.'

If they had that language! Here is the difficulty, so obvious that it escapes notice in many
panegyrics of the Muses. In the other arts there
is nothing like the curse of Babel; but the divine
Idea of Poetry, abiding the same with itself in
essence, shining with the same light, as Drummond sees it, in Homer and Virgil, Ronsard and
Garcilaso de la Vega, is actually seen by very few
votaries in each and all of those several lamps.
The light of Poetry may be all over the world
and belong to the whole human race, yet how
little of it is really available, compared with the
other arts! It is broken up among the various
languages, and in such a way that not even time
and study can always be trusted to find the true
idea of Poetry. It is not merely that you are
required to spend on the tongues the time that
might be given to bear-baiting (as Sir Andrew
discovered, ancestor of so many old gentlemen
whose education has been neglected, so many
seekers of culture), but even when you have
mastered the grammar and dictionary you may
find in the foreign poets insuperable difficulties
of thought and sentiment. For poetic melody is
not the same thing as music; it is much more
deeply idiomatic and national. French is better

understood in this country, more widely read than any foreign language ; yet even the poets in this country, some of them, have spoken dismal things in disparagement of French poetry. It is no uncommon thing for ingenuous youth, lovers of poetry in England, to be made unhappy by the difficulty and strangeness, as it seems to them, of French verse. Mr. John Bailey and Mr. Eccles have helped them, and you remember how our friend, M. Émile Legouis, came here nine years ago and dealt faithfully with the English poets and critics who boasted of their deafness. They were refuted and confounded, their injustice exposed with logical wit, their grudging objections overborne simply by the advocate's voice, as he read the songs of Musset's *Fortunio* and Victor Hugo's *Fantine*.[1]

But the difficulties remain, and English readers have to be taught that the French Alexandrine is neither ' our four-footed verse of the triple cadence ' nor yet what the Northern languages made of it in the seventeenth century, High Dutch or Low Dutch, and Danish ; and Drayton in *Polyolbion* :

Through the Dorsetian fields that lie in open view
My progress I again must seriously pursue.

[1] *Défense de la poésie française, à l'usage des lecteurs anglais.* (Constable, 1912.)

The peculiar idiom of the French tongue is diffused through all French poetry, and if this makes it hard for us, what becomes of the universal pattern which Drummond holds up as the same for all nations—'like the Ancients, and conform to those rules which hath been agreed unto by all times' ? What is the use of all times agreeing, if each nation hears nothing but its own tune ?

On the other hand, Drummond's worship of the Muses is not to be dismissed as fashionable rhetoric or conventional idealism. He knew what he was talking about, and he is thinking naturally of his own well-studied verse, his own share in the service of true poetry, along with Petrarch, Ronsard, Boscan, and Garcilaso. The names are not chosen at random, they are not there for ornament, like historical allusions of the popular preacher gabbling 'Socrates, Buddha, and Emerson', or like the formula of 'Goethe, Kant, and Beethoven', that used to pester us in the enlightened journalism of the War. When Drummond names Petrarch, Bartas, Ronsard, Boscan, and Garcilaso, he means the poets whom he knows and follows ; more particularly in the Italian and Spanish names he means an art of poetry which he has made his own. For Drummond of Hawthornden belongs, like Spenser and

Milton, to the great tradition of the Renaissance in modern poetry, the most comprehensive and vitally effective school of poetry in Christendom after the mediaeval fashion of Provence which it succeeds and continues. Drummond knows that he belongs to the great company of artists in poetry who get their instruction from Italy, and he is right : his sonnets and madrigals are part of that Italian school which transformed the poetry of France and England, Portugal and Spain ; which gave to England the music of Spenser's *Epithalamion* and of *Lycidas*. The difficulties of the curse of Babel are not abolished ; but it is matter of historical fact that Italian poetry got over those obstacles in the sixteenth century ; in some places even earlier. The Italian measures and modes of thought are adopted in other countries. Garcilaso and Camoens are Italian poets writing Castilian and Portuguese. Their names are found together in that pretty scene near the end of *Don Quixote* ; the shepherdesses who took Don Quixote out of their silken fowling-nets were going to act eclogues of Garcilaso and Camoens. Drummond's madrigals, Milton's verses *On Time*, are pure Italian form. The poets of that tradition or school, or whatever it may be called, are not talking wildly, they are not hypocrites, if they speak as Drummond does of Poetry and say 'she subsisteth by herself, and after one demeanour and continuance her beauty appeareth to all ages '. At any rate they have proved in their own practice that they agree in different languages, drawing the same pattern, following the same rules of thought and melody.

With this reality in their mind they are justified to themselves in arguing that Poetry has not to be invented anew and is not to be trifled with. Drummond in his respect for authority is quite different from the mere critics who preach up the Ancients. Any one can do that. We know their dramatic unities, and their receipts to make an epic poem. But the poet who belongs to a great tradition of art, transcending local barriers of language, is in a different case altogether. Even though he may not be, as Drummond was not himself, one of the great masters, and though the forms of his poetry be no more varied than those of Petrarch, still he has the reality of his own poems. The merely intellectual scheme of the critic turns to reality in the practical reason of the poet. His poetic life is larger than himself, and it is real life. Abstract and ideal in one way, no doubt, if you think of a bodiless Petrarchian form, identical in all the imitators of Petrarch. But the empty abstract Italian form of verse, the

unbodied ghost of sonnets and *canzoni*, is itself
real and a source of life :

> Small at first, and weak and frail
> Like the vapour of the vale :

but ' thoughts sprang where'er that step did fall ',
in the dance of the Italian syllables. The life of
the poet is real in the poems he composes ;
through them he knows where he is ; his praise
of universal poetry is what he has made true for
himself in the moments of his life, which he
shares somehow with Petrarch and the other
poets. Drummond has not had as good fortune
as they, though before we leave him let us
remember that Charles Lamb has put Drummond
among the best-loved names. Drummond is in the
great tradition, and this is what he makes of it :

> Rouse Memnon's mother from her Tython's bed,
> That she thy carrier may with roses spread,
> The nightingales thy coming each where sing,
> Make an eternal spring,
> Give life to this dark world which lieth dead.

And again :

> This world is made a hell
> Depriv'd of all that in it did excel ;
> O Pan, Pan, winter is fallen in our May,
> Turn'd is in night our day.

It is the tune of Petrarch, Garcilaso, and Camoens,
of the prevalent Italian school. It is poetry, as

the art of poetry was understood for two or three centuries, in Italy and wherever the Italian poets found an audience.

What is there in it ? When one looks into it to find the common element, to abstract the quintessence of the Italian school, is there anything more important than their favourite form of verse ? Namely, that harmony of their longer and shorter lines which Dante explained in his essay on the principles of Italian poetry—the harmony of our ten-syllable and six-syllable line, which in Italian is eleven and seven. Of which Dante says (with strange enthusiasm over a very simple metrical formula, you will think) :

' The most noble verse, which is the hendecasyllable, if it be accompanied with the verse of seven, yet so as still to keep the pre-eminence, will be found exulting higher still in light and glory.'

Et licet hoc (i.e. endecasyllabum) quod dictum est celeberrimum carmen ut dignum est videatur omnium aliorum, si eptasyllabi aliqualem societatem assumat, dummodo principatum obtineat, clarius magisque sursum superbire videtur ; sed hoc ulterius elucidandum remaneat.

Whatever else there may be in the Art of Poetry, there is this mysterious power of certain formulas, abstract relations of syllables ; of all these frames of verse in modern poetry there is none of greater dignity and at the same time more widely spread, more generally understood than this measure of the Italian *Canzone*. A bodiless thing ; in itself you would say as abstract as a geometrical diagram and of not much more worth for poetry. Yet read the great lyrical poems of Spenser and Milton, read the *Ode to a Nightingale*, *The Scholar Gipsy*, *Thyrsis*, and you will hear how the abstract harmony takes possession of the minds of poets, and compels their thought and imagination to move in the same measure. The noblest thoughts have gone to this tune :

> Fame is no plant that grows on mortal soil
> Nor in the glistering foil
> Set off to the world nor in broad rumour lies.

Our own poet of *Thyrsis* makes a contrast between his world, the Cumnor hills, the Wytham flats, the upper river, and the Sicilian fields of the old pastoral poetry :

> When Dorian shepherds sang to Proserpine.

Yet his Oxford verse is derived from Italy, from the poetry that began at the court of the Norman kings in Sicily : ' Flowers first open'd on Sicilian air '.

In Drummond's praise of poetry we can detect two modes of thought, equally true but not equally effective. One is regard for the Ancients, which we can all share as readers of poetry. The

other mode is adherence to a certain noble tradition of verse which is a living influence much
nearer to the mind of the artist. Looking at
Homer and Virgil, he is in a theatre along with
innumerable other spectators. But at the sound
of Petrarch's verse, he leaves the benches and
takes his place in the orchestra. The infinite
riches of Homer and Virgil he appreciates as
a man of taste and a scholar; but the simple
Italian metrical formula—11 : 7—makes a poet
of him.

I have long thought of writing a book on the
measures of modern poetry, from about the year
1100, when it begins in Provence. Whether it
would do for lectures, I am not sure. It might
possibly be useful if not entertaining. You will
allow me a quotation, which I hope is not impertinent; a passage from the life of Dr. William
Crowe, of New College, who was Public Orator
a hundred years ago; a poet of whom Wordsworth thought well, and the author of a treatise
on versification. 'Writing to Rogers in Feb-
ruary, 1827, to ask him to negotiate with Murray
for the issue of a new edition of his poems, in
which he wished to include a treatise on English
versification, Crowe says :

  " If he is willing to undertake the publishing I will
  immediately furnish more particulars and also submit

the copy to your inspection. If the part on versification could be out before the middle of April it would find a present sale in Oxford, for this reason : there are above four score young poets who start every year for the English prize, and as I am one of the five judges to decide it they would (many of them) buy a copy to know my doctrine on the subject. The compositions are delivered in about the beginning of May." ' [1]

My treatise will, I think, bring out some curious things, not generally known, of the same sort as the well ascertained and widespread influence of the Italian *Canzone* on the solemn odes of many languages. The same magical life of the spirit of verse is found everywhere. The best in this kind are echoes, and they travel over prodigious distances. My story will begin with the Venerable Bede, the first Englishman to write on prosody. Ages before the English took to the measures of modern verse Bede explained in Latin how it would be done. He shows the difference between learned and popular, metrical and rhythmical verse; how without respect for quantity the measure of strict verse may be imitated, and how the rustic licence of popular poets may be used by artists in poetry. He gives the rule (e.g.) of the trochaic tetrameter;

[1] Clayden, *Rogers and his Contemporaries*, ii. 29.

trochaic and tetrameter still, he reckons it, even when the rules of metrical quantity are neglected :

Apparebit repentina dies magna Domini.

A thousand years later the tune of it takes the mind of Dr. Johnson, and he sings :

> Long-expected one and twenty,
>   Ling'ring year, at length is flown :
> Pride and pleasure, pomp and plenty,
>   Great *Sir John*, are now your own.

> Loosen'd from the minor's tether,
>   Free to mortgage or to sell,
> Wild as wind and light as feather,
>   Bid the sons of thrift farewell.

It appears first in modern poetry in William of Poitiers. His authorship of Burns's favourite stanza is well known. He also uses this, the verse of *a Toccata of Galuppi*, combined with the verse of *Love among the Ruins*.

When Captain Scott Moncrieff the other day translated the *Song of Roland* in the verse of the original, he found the measure recognized as that of the old Scottish version of the 124th Psalm :

> Now Israel may say and that truly
> If that the LORD had not our cause maintained.

The reason is that the Scottish poet was translating from the French Psalter of Marot and Beza ; he wanted the French tune for his

congregation of ' Gude and godlie ballads ', and
of course he had to keep the measure with the
sharp pause at the fourth syllable, just as in
Roland :

Halt sunt li pui e tenebrus e grant

and

En Rencesvals mult grant est la dulur.

For a thousand years in Christendom the Art
of Poetry has lived on the old forms of rhythmical verse, derived, some of them obviously,
others otherwise, from the metres of Greek and
Latin, with the help of musical tunes.

Now this seems to bring out a considerable
difference between the art of poetry and the
other arts, at any rate in modern times. We talk
of schools of poetry ; but the beginners in poetry
do not work through their apprenticeship in
schools of art and offices like students of painting,
music, and architecture. They are not taught ;
they have much to learn, but they learn it in their
own way ; the rudiments are easily acquired.
Even a momentous discovery like that of which
Dante speaks, the Italian harmony, as I have
called it, is a trivial thing in appearance ; it has
been the life of very glorious poems, but there
is nothing in it that needs to be explained to
a working poet.

Is it true, or not, that the great triumphs of

poetical art often come suddenly ? Art like that
of Pindar would seem to be impossible without
long preparation ; but the Drama in Athens,
England, and Spain, does it not seem to come
very suddenly by its own, and attain its full proportions almost at once when once it has begun ?
The speed of the victory in England has been
rather obscured for the popular mind through the
conspiracy of Shakespeare's friends and admirers
to praise him in the wrong way for native uncor-
rected genius, not at all for art. Yet is there anything more amazing in Shakespeare's life than
his security in command of theatrical form ? One
of the first things he does, when he has a little
leisure, is to invent the comedy of idle good
manners in *Love's Labour 's Lost* ; in *A Midsummer Night's Dream* he raises and completes
the finest and most varied structure of poetical
comedy : where did he learn it all ? There had
been nothing on earth like it ; what had Plautus
or Terence to contribute to that entertainment
of Theseus and Hippolyta ? Did Shakespeare get
anything from classical comedy except the *Errors*
and that fardel of baby things which proves the
parentage of Perdita ? That eternal bag of
evidences—πηρίδιον γνωρισμάτων—it was a disappoint-
ment lately to observe that Menander could not
leave it behind him when he was brought up from

underground in Egypt. Shakespeare and Molière
(in *Scapin*) have no scruples about the bundle
of tokens at the end of the play, identifying
the female infant. Yet to wait centuries for
Menander in the original Greek, and then to
find him dwelling with zest on this old fardel—it
did not add to the gaiety of nations. Shakespeare
did not need this misadventure of Menander to
bring out the contrast. Where did he learn his
incomparable art ?

On the other hand, there may be convention
and long tradition leading to a sudden stroke of
genius. Two of the most original of English
poets, Chaucer and Burns, are the most indebted
to their poetical ancestors. Burns has been
injured in the same way as Shakespeare, by the
wrong sort of admiration. Unlike Shakespeare,
he began this himself, with the voluntary humility
of his Edinburgh dedication to the Caledonian
Hunt : ' I tuned my wild artless notes as she
inspired '. ' She ' is ' the Poetic Genius of my
country '. But the Muse of Scotland had established for Burns a convention and tradition full
of art ; his book is the result of two or three
generations of poetical schooling, and ' wild
artless notes ' are as unlike the perfect style of
Burns as the sentiment of his preface generally is
unlike the ironical vision of the *Holy Fair*.

The Art of Poetry is much more free than the other arts, in the sense that the right men do not need such steady training. Perhaps it is easier for the right men to work miracles, such as Burns did, in bringing the appearance of novelty and freshness out of old fashions. Also the essence of poetry is such that often much smaller things, comparatively, tell for success than in painting or music. Eight lines beginning ' A slumber did my spirit seal ' may be larger in imagination than earth's diurnal course. Eight lines lately addressed to a mercenary army were enough to tell how the sum of things was saved :

> Their shoulders held the sky suspended,
> They stood, and earth's foundations stay.

Often single lines and phrases seem to have the value of whole poems. In the old English song Bitwene Mershe and Averill when spray beginneth to springe ' the opening words are everything ; though one is glad to have more. Herrick has put the whole meaning of the pilgrim's progress into two lines of his *Noble Numbers* :

> I kenn my home, and it affords some ease
> To see far off the smoking villages.

Quoniam advena ego sum et peregrinus, sicut omnes patres mei. It is the English landscape too, as you come down the hill at the end of the day.

Gavin Douglas, Bishop of Dunkeld, is praised
for his descriptions, particularly the Summer and
Winter in two of his prologues. He is not often
quoted for his great discovery in a line or two of
the thirteenth prologue of *Eneados*, where he tells
how he watched the midsummer midnight in the
North, and finds not only the right word for what
he sees, but the right word for his own poetry :

> Yondir down dwinis the evin sky away,
> And up springis the bricht dawing of day
> Intill ane uthir place nocht fer in sunder
> Quhilk to behald was plesance and half wonder.

He sees a new thing in the life of the world—no
poet that I know of (except Homer) had thought
of it before—and in naming it he gives the interpretation also, the spirit of poetry : plesance, and
half wonder.

This sort of miracle, this sudden glory, is an
escape from the fashion of the time, and the
fashions of poetry, the successive schools are
such that escapes are not so difficult as in the
other arts. The history of poetry must be the
history of schools and fashions. But the progress
of poesy does not mean simply the refutation of
old schools by new fashions. The poets have
sometimes thought so ; like Keats in *Hyperion*,
possibly ; like Dante when he speaks of the older
lyric poetry as distained by comparison with the

sweet new style, *dolce stil nuovo*, of his own masters and fellows. But apart from the grace that you may find in the older fashion as a whole, taking it as an antiquarian curiosity, there is the chance, the certainty, that here and there among the old songs you will come upon something new, independent, a miracle. In the old lyric poetry of Provence, which has been made a byword for conventionality and monotonous repetition, there are poems that seem to start afresh, worth dwelling on and remembering. This is true also of the other similar school of the German minnesingers, which has been equally maligned.

Mnemosyne, Mother of the Muses, has allowed many things to pass into oblivion. But the Memory of the World in poetry keeps alive everything that is kept at all, and in such a way that at any time it may turn to something new. The simplest measures of verse, the best known stories, you can never be sure that they are out of date. The stories of the Greek mythology have long ago been indexed. I have an old Dutch Ovid in prose, the *Metamorphosis* translated ' for the behoof of all noble spirits and artists, such as rhetoricians, painters, engravers, goldsmiths, &c.' Nothing could be more business-like : a handy book of suitable subjects then ; now long abandoned, you would say, in the

march of intellect.   Yet we know how the old
tragic legend of Procne and Philomela turned
into the *Itylus* of *Poems and Ballads* :

> O sweet stray sister, O shifting swallow,
>> The heart's division divideth us ;
>>> Thy heart is light as a leaf of a tree,
> But mine goes forth among sea-gulfs hollow
>> To the place of the slaying of Itylus,
>>> The feast of Daulis, the Thracian sea.

There is no need for me to say more of this :

> *Who hath remembered, who hath forgotten ?*

For the present, I have spoken long enough.

Note.—This lecture was printed separately in 1920.
I am indebted to Mr. T. R. Mills for correction of
a mistake on p. 21 : the author of the ' old 124th ' was
William Whittingham, sometime Fellow of All Souls
and Dean of Durham.

SHELLEY

THE history of poetry, the history of all art, is a dangerous trade for those that practise it; the critic is apt to think himself superior to the objects of his vision and discourse, he is rashly induced to treat the procession of poets as if he had the management of it all. He ought to be ashamed of himself and to offer sacrifices in deprecation of the Mighty Powers. The right way of thinking, a contrast to the historian's attitude of confidence and command, is Browning's at the beginning of *Sordello*—overcome and abashed at the thought that Shelley might possibly be there, among his audience :

> . . . stay—thou, spirit, come not near
> Now—not this time desert thy cloudy place
> To scare me, thus employed, with that pure face !
> I need not fear this audience, I make free
> With them, but then this is no place for thee !
> The thunder-phrase of the Athenian, grown
> Up out of memories of Marathon,
> Would echo like his own sword's griding screech
> Braying a Persian shield,—the silver speech
> Of Sidney's self, the starry paladin,
> Turn intense as a trumpet sounding in
> The knights to tilt,—wert thou to hear !

How mean and poor in comparison with this reverence is the biographer pronouncing judgement, the critic enumerating tendencies and playing with the spirit of the age, or studying the poet's *Belesenheit*, as the Germans conveniently call it—i. e. all the books that the poet is known to have read—in order to find where the music comes from. 'We take upon us the mystery of things as if we were God's spies.' This is Keats's quotation, telling of the life of Burns, and recognizing what vanity there is in the attempt to come to a conclusion, or even to have an opinion at all in such a matter as that.

Shelley has done something to justify the historian and his processes : he speaks himself of the spirit of the age, and in the preface to the *Revolt of Islam* he states, I think for the first time clearly, what is now a commonplace of literary history—the relation of the individual poet to the common fashion of his time :

'I have avoided, as I have said before, the imitation of any contemporary style. But there must be a resemblance, which does not depend upon their own will, between all the writers of any particular age. They cannot escape from subjection to a common influence which arises out of an infinite combination of circumstances belonging to the times in which they live, though each is in a degree the author of the very influence by which his being is thus pervaded. Thus,

the tragic Poets of the age of Pericles; the Italian
revivers of ancient learning; those mighty intellects
of our own country that succeeded the Reformation,
the translators of the Bible, Shakspeare, Spenser, the
Dramatists of the reign of Elizabeth, and Lord Bacon;
the colder spirits of the interval that succeeded;—all
resemble each other, and differ from every other in
their several classes. In this view of things, Ford can
no more be called the imitator of Shakspeare, than
Shakspeare the imitator of Ford. There were perhaps
few other points of resemblance between these two
men, than that which the universal and inevitable
influence of their age produced. And this is an
influence which neither the meanest scribbler, nor the
sublimest genius of any era, can escape; and which
I have not attempted to escape.'

There is some excuse for taking Shelley at his
word. He has told the reading public what he
thinks about the education of a poet; he has
given his own theory of literary history, and thus
challenged the critic to test it. When he tells
us in prose how his life has trained him for poetry,
it is not impertinent to ask for more particulars.
'The Poet is least lyar', Sidney says; but the
poet has often a magnificent way of dealing with
biographical facts; when he gives you facts, he
cannot complain if they are scrutinized. Here
is part of Shelley's story of his life from that same
preface :

'The circumstances of my accidental education have

been favourable to this ambition. I have been familiar from boyhood with mountains and lakes, and the sea, and the solitude of forests : Danger, which sports upon the brink of precipices, has been my playmate. I have trodden the glaciers of the Alps, and lived under the eye of Mont Blanc. I have been a wanderer among distant fields. I have sailed down mighty rivers, and seen the sun rise and set, and the stars come forth, whilst I have sailed night and day down a rapid stream among mountains.'

' In what year of our Lord was this ? ' said my uncle Toby. It sounds at first too large, but it is not more nor less than true history ; it is proved in the narrative of the six weeks' tour. The rivers are not the imaginary floods of *Alastor* ; they are the Reuss and the Rhine ; the voyage was adventurous enough between Lucerne and Bonn. Incidentally Mrs. Shelley reports that Shelley knocked down another passenger who was making himself offensive in a discussion over deck chairs in a language which Shelley did not understand. To supplement the Preface out of the printed and published Tour is not only not impertinent ; it is a right and proper attention to the poet's story, and it shows the story to be no more than the truth. Then when Shelley speaks of himself as sharing in the general poetic fashion of his own time, it cannot be wrong to ask what that fashion is, or how we are to think

of the modes of poetry prevalent thus for a time,
and then passing away.

' The spirit of the age ! ' Shelley is the first
author quoted for that phrase in the *New English
Dictionary*. ' March of intellect ' is in a letter
of Keats some years earlier than the first quotation
in the *Dictionary*. And Keats in *Sleep and Poetry*
speaks of

> The shiftings of the mighty winds that blow
> Hither and thither all the changing thoughts
> Of man.

It is good evidence of the power of common
fashions of thought that Keats and Shelley at the
same time, independently, should be thinking of
the spiritual life of the world as a succession
of periods, each with its own imaginative and
intellectual gifts and character. To both poets
the idea of progress is immensely important, for
their own lives, and their theory of life, and
for the substance of their poetry, especially in
Prometheus and *Hyperion*. Both of them translate
philosophy into poetry, if we may use the name
philosophy, as I think we may, not only for the
argument of Godwin's *Political Justice*, but for
Keats's description of his own life in that well-
known letter to J. H. Reynolds.

Sometimes one is inclined to think of Shelley as
distracted between prose argument and poetry,

uncertain which to follow : the preface to *Prometheus* announces a scheme of a philosophical work :

> ' Should I live to accomplish what I purpose, that is, produce a systematical history of what appear to me to be the genuine elements of human society, let not the advocates of injustice and superstition flatter themselves that I should take Aeschylus rather than Plato as my model.'

We are inclined to take Keats, on the other hand, as thinking always poetically : so that abstract thought with him is always one with imagery and musical language, that is to say, *not* abstract. Yet this is not always so : Keats is good at analytical reasoning, and in the argument of the often quoted letter to Reynolds it is possible to find the argument of *Hyperion*. Keats can debate and explain, and *Hyperion* is not pure imagination. It is allegory, like *Prometheus*, a poetical version of thoughts which had been for a long time in the poet's mind, not always as poetry. Both poets are reflective and philosophical, and the philosophy of both of them is a philosophy of history, of the march of intellect, the changing spirit of the age. This is the meaning of the moral of *Hyperion*, clearly expressed in the speech of Oceanus, clearly in the letter to Reynolds (May 1818), particularly in the sentences about Milton.

Keats has given his simile of human life as he perceives it :

'I compare Human Life to a large mansion of many apartments, two of which I can only describe, the doors of the rest being as yet shut upon me.'

He comes to the end of the second room into the darkness, where many doors are open :

'but all dark—all leading to dark passages. To this point was Wordsworth come, as far. as I can conceive, when he wrote *Tintern Abbey*, and it seems to me that his genius is explorative of those dark passages. Now if we live and go on thinking we too shall explore them. He is a genius and superior to us in so far as he can, more than we, make discoveries and shed a light on them. Here I must think Wordsworth is deeper than Milton, though I think it has depended more on the general and gregarious advance of intellect than individual greatness of mind.

. . . .

[Milton] did not think into the human heart as Wordsworth has done. Yet Milton as a philosopher had sure as great powers as Wordsworth. What is then to be inferred? O many things. It proves that there is really a grand march of intellect, it proves that a mighty Providence subdues the mightiest minds to the service of the time being, whether it be in human knowledge or religion. . . .'

I have quoted these passages from Keats because the difference between the two poets is so striking that it ought not to be exaggerated. The difference is not that Shelley is a philosopher and Keats a purely imaginative artist. Keats can think well enough in prose when he wants to do so. The difference is that Keats's progress is straightforward through his three volumes— breaking through, from *Endymion* to *Hyperion* and the odes, carried on by a poetical logic which detects the fallacies of *Endymion* and goes on to more secure ground and more coherent work. The wavering uncertainty of his last days does nothing to detract from the volume of 1820.

Shelley's poetical life cannot be represented as continuous steady advance. His mind was divided, and though his conquests in the region of poetry are secure, they are gained through many distractions. He had too many things to think about, and too many ways of thinking. He was tossed to and fro by many winds of doctrine, often too obedient to the spirit of the age. He was easily led, and his judgement was uncertain. Of course, in his childhood he was captured by the school of *Horrid Mysteries* ; he could not help it. Has any assiduous researcher for a Doctor's degree, or any other form of the apparent good, written a dissertation on *the Skull* in poetry and

romance in the eighteenth century ? There is
plenty of material :

> ' On a sudden Ginotti's frame mouldered to a
> gigantic skeleton, yet two pale and ghastly flames
> glared in his eyeless sockets.'

The explorer will do well not to neglect France,
where ' la tête de mort ' had a spell of dominion
about the same time.

Shelley's early romances are shocking examples,
though not too ridiculous to be reprinted. He
was a great novel-reader. The rocks and chasms
of *Alastor* have been closely compared with the
mountain scenery in a novel, *Celestina*, by
Mrs. Charlotte Smith. My old friend, Henry
Sweet, made this comparison in detail, without
pressing it too far ; he was a very strict philo-
logist who was a lover of romance and of Shelley's
poetry. His essay will be found in the *Furnivall
Miscellany*. Shelley did not need Mrs. Charlotte
Smith to tell him what precipices were like, and
he did not need any cliffs or cataracts to teach
him admiration or horror. The strangest landscape and most foreign could not have affected
him more than what he saw walking out from
Oxford one grey winter afternoon :

> ' I was walking with a friend in the neighbourhood
> of that city, engaged in earnest and interesting

conversation. We suddenly turned the corner of a lane, and the view which its high banks and hedges had concealed presented itself. The view consisted of a windmill standing in one among many plashy meadows enclosed with stone walls, the irregular and broken ground between the wall and the road in which we stood ; a long low hill behind the windmill, and a gray covering of uniform cloud spread over the evening sky. I suddenly remembered to have seen that exact scene in some dream. . . .'

There he breaks off ; it is too much for him. There is more ghostly terror for him in that dull November landscape than in all the gorges of *Alastor*. But to the end of his life he is subject to the fascination of romantic scenery, and spends time on it for its own sake. He does not return to *Tales of Terror and Wonder*, though of course he appreciates Mrs. Shelley's *Frankenstein* ; and he would have been interested in the after life of Byron's *Vampire*.

Shelley's early verse in *St. Irvyne* is so bad that a theory of demoniac possession by a dull devil is the simplest way of accounting for the pheno-mena ; with, naturally, a theory of divine inspiration to explain what followed—though it is not all bad verse followed by all good ; his poetical sense wavers—*Queen Mab*, not very long after *St. Irvyne*, is carefully written on respectable models, and copies *Samson Agonistes* and the

Italian pastoral choruses. Much of Shelley's later verse is technically not so good as *Queen Mab*.

In his philosophical arguments I think it is possible to show a similar wavering. Not all the positions gained are held strongly. I will offer here a description of the *Defence of Poetry*, and ask whether it does not surrender ground which Shelley had won for himself in original speculation upon human life. Let me begin upon the stronger ground, as it seems to me, in the earlier moral essay, 1815, the fragment of a treatise on Morals. There Shelley discovers that what the student of morals has to attend to is the differences, not the resemblances, among men and actions. The minute particulars of character and action are what makes the man. There appears to be a glimmering of this truth in Aristotle's *Ethics*, where he introduces those very pleasant satirical descriptions of bad characters, thus persuading some of his readers that they have his authority for believing in novels as the most satisfactory kind of moral philosophy.

Shelley writes thus, in 1815 :

> ‘ Each individual who composes the vast multitude which we have been contemplating, has a peculiar frame of mind which, while the features of the great mass of his actions remain uniform, impresses the minuter lineaments with its peculiar hues. Thus,

whilst his life as a whole is like the lives of other men, in detail it is most unlike, and the more subdivided the actions become; that is, the more they enter into that class which have a vital influence on the happiness of others and his own, so much the more are they distinct from those of other men :

> Those little nameless unremembered acts
> Of kindness and of love,

as well as those deadly outrages which are inflicted by a look, a word—or less—the very refraining from some faint and most evanescent expression of countenance, these flow from a profounder source than the series of an habitual conduct, which, it has been already said, derives its origin from without. . . . The deepest abyss of these vast and multitudinous caverns it is necessary that we should visit.'

Now you might suppose that Shelley's appreciation of individual differences would make it utterly impossible for him to see any good in the pure Ideal Hero. But in the *Defence of Poetry* he seems to go quite to the other extreme from his *Fragment on Morals*. He is not content with the heroes of Homer until he has apologized for those failings which make them the characters we know. He sees in Achilles a perfect hero disguised as a revengeful man, and speaks as if Homer had condescended to this disguise :

' Few poets of the highest class have chosen to exhibit the beauty of their conceptions in its naked

truth and splendour ; and it is doubtful whether this
alloy of costume, habit, etc., be not necessary to temper
this planetary music for mortal ears.'

Is not this very like the Ideal of Sir Joshua
Reynolds's grand style, in contrast to the expressive
significance of the mere portrait ? Is it not the
old abstract classical ideal of the Renaissance ?
It reminds one of the way in which Achilles and
Hector were exhibited as models for authors of
romance, to take the place of Amadis and Pal-
merin. Noble indeed is Shelley's *Defence of
Poetry* ; to all ingenuous minds an enthralling
argument, a revelation of a real world of beauty.
But it wants the *Fragment on Morals* to complete
it ; to remind the reader that life is not all
generalities, and (in this connexion) that poetry,
like the law of England, is a very particular
thing.

There is danger in Shelley's *Defence of Poetry*.
Its enthusiastic worship of poetry is so persuasive
that it may pass with some readers as a substitute
for poetry itself, and leave them satisfied that they
know all about it, though they know nothing else.
Do we never meet lovers of Poetry who believe
in it (like some lovers of Education) as something
to be earnestly recommended to every one else ?
Shelley, of course, is far beyond that danger,
being a poet himself, and also one of the most

devoted readers of poetry. He did not know
everything all at once. A hundred and more
years ago, when he and Hogg met as freshmen in
the Hall of University, at the beginning of
Michaelmas Term, they started a discussion on
the rival merits of German and Italian poetry,
and ended by confessing that neither knew anything about either of them. Ten years later
Shelley had been deep in German, Italian,
Spanish, and he writes about his reading with the
gusto of Charles Lamb or Hazlitt. Ought any one
to take up Shelley's *Defence of Poetry* until he
understands why Shelley translated the *Cyclops*
of Euripides, and the Homeric *Hymn to Mercury*,
or what he thought of Calderon—' bathing in
the light and odour of the starry and flowery
Autos ' ?

Shelley's philosophical *Defence of Poetry* is not
itself Poetry, and Shelley would not have us think
so. But it is one mode in which he expresses
a theory which is expressed poetically in *Prometheus* and *Adonais*. The prose meaning of the
Defence is the poetical meaning of Asia and
Urania. Some readers of Shelley, it may be
suspected, are content with the prose meaning.
The worst of philosophical and religious poetry
is that it is apt to put religion or philosophy in
the place of poetry. Philosophical vision may be

poetical vision in the mind of the poet ; but if it be philosophical, i.e. scientific, it is capable of statement in prose. Wordsworth's theory of the Universe cannot refuse to be compared with such prose statements as William James has compiled in his *Aspects of Religious Consciousness* from American prose authors in tune with the Infinite, Mr. Blood, Mr. Buck, Mr. Starbuck, and Mr. Trine. In making such a comparison we are not happy, we cannot say that a divine pleasure, *quaedam divina voluptas*, comes over our minds. We are troubled by the likeness ; we resent what seems the intrusion of prose into what Wordsworth had made the substance of his philosophic poetry. Shelley in his *Defence* goes some way to remove the landmarks of Poetry. ' He who would do good to another ', said Blake in full agreement with Shelley's earlier moral essay, ' must do it in minute particulars. General good is the refuge of the scoundrel, the hypocrite, and the flatterer.' Shelley's *Defence of Poetry* is too like this ' general good '. It might afford a living to professors of poetry who do not care for any particular poetical tune.

He is clearer and more satisfactory in the preface to *Prometheus* which has been already quoted, where he distinguishes the kinds and keeps prose argument for its proper work. His

own prose is rational and business-like. But there
is this difficulty for him at a certain point in his
life, that he has a theory in his mind which may
be stated in prose, for which, at the same time,
he wishes to find a proper poetical form. He
wishes to put the Idea of Revolution into poetry,
epic or lyric or drama, and he is troubled and goes
wrong because the form does not spring at once
to answer and obey him. He writes *Laon and
Cythna*, the *Revolt of Islam*, the epic of Revolution. Is it rude to say that he fails ? It is his
own opinion ; and he tries again. The right
form comes to him : *Prometheus Unbound.* The
poetical truth of the Greek fable gives him the
form and frame he requires. The cumbersome
romantic heroic machine of the *Revolt of Islam* is
dismissed to ' the lumber room of oblivion '.
Here in its place are the Ocean nymphs of
Aeschylus to help him and Prometheus. His
own mythology which had been buried in the
epic has now free play :

> The world's great age begins anew,
> The golden years return.

Let me read Macaulay on Shelley ; let me
salute the first poet who went out of his way to
speak with understanding of Shelley's mythology.
The passage no doubt is familiar ; at the same
time it is a surprise—breaking out suddenly where

you do not expect it, a digression in a review of the *Pilgrim's Progress* :

' The strong imagination of Shelley made him an idolator in his own despite. Out of the most indefinite terms of a hard, cold, dark, metaphysical system, he made a gorgeous Pantheon, full of beautiful, majestic, and life-like forms. He turned atheism itself into a mythology, rich with visions as glorious as the gods that live in the marble of Phidias, or the virgin saints that smile on us from the canvass of Murillo. The Spirit of Beauty, the Principle of Good, the Principle of Evil, when he treated of them, ceased to be abstractions. They took shape and colour. They were no longer mere words; but " intelligible forms " ; " fair humanities " ; objects of love, of adoration, or of fear.

. . . .

' Some of the metaphysical and ethical theories of Shelley were certainly most absurd and pernicious. But we doubt whether any modern poet has possessed in an equal degree some of the highest qualities of the great ancient masters. The words bard and inspiration, which seem so cold and affected when applied to other modern writers, have a perfect propriety when applied to him.

. . . .

' Had he lived to the full age of man, he might not improbably have given to the world some great work of the very highest rank in design and execution. But alas !

ὁ Δάφνις ἔβα ῥόον· ἔκλυσε δίνα
τὸν Μώσαις φίλον ἄνδρα, τὸν οὐ Νύμφαισιν ἀπεχθῆ.

Macaulay did not think much of himself as a critic. Many critics, more subtle masters of finer shades, might not have remembered Theocritus. Macaulay, with his infallible memory and his poetic sense, has gone to the old Sicilian sources of *Lycidas* and *Adonais* to find the lucky words, the right words, of farewell for this shepherd : Daphnis, whom the nymphs and Muses loved, whom the eddying stream bore down.

Prometheus Unbound is not the same story as *Hyperion*, though like *Hyperion* it takes up the fable of successive dynasties of the gods. *Prometheus Unbound* is not a drama of progress through successive stages and modes of Beauty. It is a scheme of redemption as fixed as that of *Paradise Lost*. Only, like *Hyperion*, it looks to the future. It is the ultimate triumph of pure Reason and of the Soul of the world. Like *Hyperion*, it is a story that proves itself as poetry. It is itself the radiance that it represents in a fable.

There is a likeness in the end of the two poems. *Hyperion* is a fragment, because the story was already told at the point where it breaks off. Keats could not go farther, because his fable compelled him to bring Apollo himself upon the scene. But he had already put all he knew into the story of Saturn. The story required a new wonder, but Keats, short of being Apollo himself,

could not present that on his stage : to the
utmost of his power he had done it already, in
the yielding of Oceanus to the young god of the
sea. There was only one way left, if the story
were to be told to an end. He must try a new
mode of deeper reflection; the light of Apollo,
which could not be brought directly into the
picture, might be made intelligible through
deeper thought. So Keats began again with the
allegorical framework of the second *Hyperion*;
taking a new grip in the wrestling match with
his divine challenger, in order to bring out by
reflection what could not be given directly in
narrative.

The same sort of difficulty was found by
Shelley at the end of *Prometheus Unbound*. In
prudence, he ought to have stopped when he had
finished, at the end of Act III. There at the
beginning of the new world the drama is played
out. But Shelley would not be kept from going
farther ; he must venture everything, and do no
less than bring the sun into his picture. The
fourth Act of *Prometheus Unbound*, if it were to
succeed as Shelley meant it, would be something
more than poetic vision and melody.

Then came the *Cenci*, the most amazing in
some respects of all the works of Shelley. How
great it is as tragic poetry, I will not attempt to

explain. The wonder of it partly is that it is exactly what one would never have expected from the author. All the fallacious spirits that were always tempting Shelley into romantic excursions have here been ignored. The solid work stands on its own base. None of the author's own opinions are allowed to interfere with it. For himself he did not know how great it was; what an absolute repudiation of all the vanities of his luxurious dreams. He did not know that he had won through to imaginative and creative freedom. He falls back in *Epipsychidion* to his indulgence in a fanciful paradise : the weakness of it hardly needs the cruel biographical documents to bring it out.

How great a poet he was may be proved in minute particulars. His three best-known poems, are they not the *Cloud*, the *Skylark*, and the *Ode to the West Wind* ? Each of these gains in significance through inquiries and observations which may seem perhaps too trifling in comparison with the lofty ideas of the *Defence of Poetry*. But it is no part of the true admiration of Shelley not to pay attention to his accomplishments of verse. The verse of the *Cloud* is an old tune which he had used with no ordinary want of success in *St. Irvyne*; it was a tune that had haunted him ; at last it came right and true, through

discipline applied to feeble, childish suggestions
of melody.

It is a curious fact that the measure of the
Cloud has an attraction for Dutch poets, and is
used by one at least of the South African com-
posers.

The stanza of the *Skylark* shows what can
be done by poetic invention using well-known
elements. The measure is related to Spenserian
Miltonic experiments with the alexandrine. But
while the proper use of the alexandrine is to
complete and continue the measure of the heroic
line, Shelley uses it in a new way to complete
a measure which is seemingly trochaic, beginning
on the strong syllable :

> Keen as are the arrows
> Of that silver sphere,
> Whose intense lamp narrows
> In the white dawn clear,
> Until we hardly see, we feel that it is there.

It may be disguised iambic (I use the technical
terms, without prejudice, merely as labels to
denote what every one recognizes)—the iambic
comes out here and there among the short lines :

> We look before and after,
> And pine for what is not.

That is the full measure, easily recognizable as
the pattern first introduced into English verse

by Sidney ; it is the measure of the *Garden of Proserpine* :

> From too much love of living,
> From hope and fear set free.

But it comes in only accidentally in Shelley's poem. His shortened form of the verse does not give way ; his lyrical invention is carried through to the end, and there it remains unequalled ; it has never been repeated or imitated.

The *Ode to the West Wind* is more perfect in art than the *Cloud* or the *Skylark* ; the poetical logic more complete. The stanza is another of Shelley's inventions. It is made out of *terza rima* : four *terzine* in each stanza, with a final couplet. *Terza rima* somehow has never succeeded in English. Not even Shelley himself, not even in the *Triumph of Life*, can make it sound like Dante, or give it the fluency and the rich effect of rhyme which seems to come naturally in Italian, not only in the *Commedia*, but also in the lighter, more colloquial satiric poetry. Somehow the rhymes in English do not tell, and the verse moves slow. But Shelley in his lyrical use of it has overcome the difficulties ; he has quickened it, and the rhymes answer with full value.

It is a mythological poem, but the mythology is not that of *Prometheus* or *Adonais*. Of all English poems the nearest to it in this respect is

Collins's *Ode to Evening*. Evening and the West
Wind are living persons, but they are not transformed into symbolical corporeal shapes. The
ordinary prose reality, as you may reckon it, is there
in the evening landscape and the approaching storm.
The *Ode to the West Wind* is a prayer to a living
person; the power is known through the worship, it
is not seen as a God riding on the wings of the wind.

There are three parts or movements in the
poem. The first three stanzas are the first part,
adoration going out ; the fourth stanza is a return
of the worshipping mind to its own weakness.

> If I were a dead leaf thou mightest bear ;
> If I were a swift cloud to fly with thee ;
> A wave to pant beneath thy power, and share
>
> The impulse of thy strength, only less free
> Than thou, O uncontrollable ! If even
> I were as in my boyhood, and could be
>
> The comrade of thy wanderings over heaven,
> As then, when to outstrip the skiey speed
> Scarce seemed a vision, I would ne'er have striven
>
> As thus with thee in prayer in my sore need.
> Oh ! lift me as a wave, a leaf, a cloud !
> I fall upon the thorns of life ! I bleed !
>
> A heavy weight of hours has chained and bowed
> One too like thee : tameless, and swift, and proud.

From this humiliation the last stanza, the
third movement, rises in triumph ; the power

without is proved to be the power within, and
the poetical reasoning is complete.

> Make me thy lyre, even as the forest is :
> What if my leaves are falling like its own !
> The tumult of thy mighty harmonies
> Will take from both a deep autumnal tone,
> Sweet, though in sadness. Be thou, spirit fierce,
> My spirit ! Be thou me, impetuous one !
> Drive my dead thoughts over the universe
> Like withered leaves to quicken a new birth ;
> And, by the incantation of this verse,
> Scatter, as from an unextinguished hearth
> Ashes and sparks, my words among mankind !
> Be through my lips to unawakened earth
> The trumpet of a prophecy ! O wind,
> If winter comes, can Spring be far behind !

One simple fact may be observed in all three
poems ; they are none of them stanzas written
in dejection.

SAMSON AGONISTES

NO one can go far in the history of poetry without recognizing the power of formal and abstract ideals, especially in the age of the Renaissance. Of the empty patterns that fascinate the minds of poets there were two pre-eminent : the Heroic Poem and the classical Tragedy. The rules of Poetics, in Aristotle, Horace, and Julius Caesar Scaliger, were an inspiration to poets. Camoens, Tasso, and Milton write their epics according to the ' Receipt to make an epic poem '. The pattern of Greek tragedy, a mere frame, produced a great number of tragedies, in Latin, like those of George Buchanan, and in all the modern tongues. Milton's list of subjects for tragedy in the precious book that belongs to Trinity College, Cambridge, has inclined many to think that *Samson Agonistes* is the fulfilment of this early ambition and intention to write, not *Samson Agonistes*, but some tragedy or other. *Paradise Lost*, *Adam Unparadised*, had been subjects among others in the list, treated with some detail of *dramatis personae* and plot. Other subjects also have full sketches added to them : *Abram from Morea, Baptistes, Sodom burning.* Samson is not so favoured ; his story is quickly passed over as *Samson Pursophorus*, or *Hybristes*, or '*Samson marriing* or *Ramath Lechi*, Jud. 15 '. Then, ' *Dagonalia*, Jud. 16.'

From the list of titles and subjects for tragedy it can be made out that Milton had various interests and motives in his mind when he compiled it. It looks like a list of sacred subjects, for the Poem on a sacred subject. But Milton was not trifling when he drew out the Scenario of *Adam unparadised*, of *Abram from Morea*, of *Baptistes*, of *Sodom burning*. In *Baptistes*, in particular, we may find that tension of heroic resistance which we know later in *Paradise Regained* and in *Samson*. He really meant to take up something seriously and work it into a perfect poem. But some subjects are expressly noted as not for tragedy. *Theristria*, a pastoral out of *Ruth* ; the *Sheep shearers in Carmel* (that is the story of Nabal, Abigail, and David), a pastoral, I Sam. 25. By the time we come to ' British Troy ' and ' Scotch stories, or rather British of the North parts ', ending in *Macbeth*, is it not apparent that Milton, besides his definite inten-

tion, is doing literary experiments, looking at the
Bible and British history as Aristotle looks at the
Greek epics, to see how many dramas they con-
tain ? The list is only partly intended as memo-
randa for future, steady work on some chosen
theme. It is partly a diversion, like the eighteenth-
century amateur travelling in search of the
picturesque and making notes of landscape on his
way. The list does not really carry us very far.
Milton's tragic drama is very slightly related to
Samson Pursophorus in the catalogue ; and the
title *Dagonalia* there, does it not show, in contrast
to the later *Agonistes*, that Milton's mind was
still in those earlier days diffuse and wandering ?
He thinks of the feast of Dagon, and passes by ;
he is not yet possessed with the idea of Samson's
tragic remorse and heroic recovery. Generally
those sketches show that he was disinclined for
the tragic ordeal. *Baptistes* is an exception.
His plots for the drama of *Paradise Lost* give no
hint of the character of Satan ; his allegorical
personages—Divine Justice, Mercie, Wisdom,
Heavenly Love—his ' mask of all the evils of this
life and world ' that are to pass ' in shapes ' before
the eyes of Adam, make one think of the *Autos* of
Calderon, ' flowery and starry ', as Shelley found
them, rather than the strength of Greek tragedy.

Yet there is no doubt that Milton cherished along with the formal idea of Epic the formal idea of Tragedy ; and when he wrote *Samson* he pleased himself with the accomplishment of an old artistic ambition. The preface proves this : ' Heretofore men in highest dignity have laboured not a little to be thought able to compose a tragedy.' But we need not suppose that he was haunted by the ghosts of the unborn tragedies in his catalogue, or that it was his chief poetic aim, after *Paradise Lost*, to write the one perfect drama in English. He had another and more substantial motive for *Samson*.

It is pleasant by the way to remember that Dryden in some respects was more serious in his pursuit of the ideal form than his friend Milton. Dryden in his heroic plays was led by an ideal like Milton's : the Heroic Play was intended to be the most noble poetic thing, rising even beyond Tragedy to the rank of the Heroic Poem, of that Epic Form which was allowed to be the highest of which the human mind was capable in poetry. Dryden was more persevering than Milton, and more given to meditation and discussion of those mysteries. In spite of his readier wit and his lighter style, Dryden sometimes appears more old-fashioned than Milton in his respect for the Abstract Ideas of poetry. *Samson Agonistes* was not written merely as an experiment in Greek poetic form. It was written because the Greek form was the right form for something that Milton wanted to say. This is what the present argument is intended to maintain. In *Samson Agonistes* Milton is able to express himself fully, his poetic strength and fire at their utmost pitch, his genius undistracted. He finds in the form of Greek tragedy exactly the right measure and mode for something not yet accomplished in his epic poems.

Dr. Johnson thought that *Samson Agonistes* has been too much admired : ' This is the tragedy which ignorance has admired, and bigotry applauded.'

Not all critics admire it thoroughly. The late Mr. Mark Pattison, sometime Rector of Lincoln, in his Life of Milton for the *English Men of Letters* series (edited by Mr. John Morley) permits himself to say that ' as a composition the drama is languid, nerveless, occasionally halting, never brilliant '. ' In *Paradise Regained* we are conscious of a purposed restraint of strength. The simplicity of its style is an experiment, an essay of a new theory of poetic words. The simplicity of *Samson Agonistes* is a flagging of the forces, a drying

up of the rich sources from which had once
flowed the golden stream of suggestive phrase
which makes *Paradise Lost* a unique monument
of the English language. I could almost fancy
that the consciousness of decay utters itself in
the lines (594)

> I feel my genial spirits droop.'

And then Mr. Pattison quotes what I will not
repeat in this degrading context, the noblest
lines in English poetry, as proof of Milton's
flagging energy. Let me take, instead of this,
Johnson's quotation of the same passage, and then
it will be no dishonour or disgrace to repeat the
words of Milton. In the *Rambler*, No. 140, in
the second of two papers severely criticizing
Milton's tragedy, some merit is allowed to certain
passages : 'It is not easy to give a stronger
representation of the weariness of despondency
than in the words of Samson to his father—

> I feel my genial spirits droop,
> My hopes all flat : Nature within me seems
> In all her functions weary of herself ;
> My race of glory run, and race of shame,
> And I shall shortly be with them that rest.'

Johnson, who does not approve of the construction
of the tragedy, has too much sense to take the

dejection of the hero for evidence of depression in the poet. He knows that the representation of weakness here is particularly strong. If he does not say more, we need not think that this is all he knew. As for ourselves, we will go on wondering whether anything finer than those verses was ever written by Milton or any other mortal man. As for Mr. Pattison, I think we may leave him. In that same book he shows, on an earlier page, first that he could not read *L'Allegro* for himself, secondly that he could not understand the syntax when it was explained to him. But these disparaging notes, I need hardly say, are not intended to deny Mr. Pattison's literary skill in writing elegantly about the lives of great scholars.

Milton was driven by the strength of his own genius to write the tragedy of *Samson*. Till that was done he had not uttered himself to the full. Let me tell what happened, as it appears to me.

When Milton was advised by Thomas Ellwood that he had still to speak of *Paradise Found*, he was silent for a time, in a muse, as Ellwood tells us. What he was musing about our Merton Professor has guessed. Partly, on the stupidity of Thomas Ellwood. Indeed it was going rather far, even for that irrepressible young Quaker, to

tax Milton with forgetting the Redemption in
the poem of the Fall of Man. But Milton had
other things to muse upon besides the limitations
of Thomas Ellwood. He was not fully satisfied
with his great poem. He did not indeed feel the
quaintness of it as Chaucer or Dante would have
felt the childishness of Milton's scenery. *Oltre
la spera che più larga gira*, beyond the highest
sphere, you come with Milton, not like Dante to
the mind of God, but to the Paradise of Fools
in a dry, parched, and god-forsaken land on the
outside of the fixed stars ; and then to an enor-
mous repetition of the Homeric universe, Heaven
above and Hell below, only wanting the old
familiar flat earth in between. It is not always
recognized that the seventeenth century is the
quaintest age in history ; the emblem pictures
are the true fashion of the time, and Milton and
Dryden have their share in it : Milton, for
example, with the compasses of the Creator :

> He took the golden compasses, prepared
> In God's eternal store, to circumscribe
> This universe, and all created things :
> One foot he centred, and the other turn'd
> Round through the vast profundity obscure—

Dryden with the heavenly extinguisher that puts
out the fire of London. But it is not likely that

Milton felt remorse for anything in the scenery
or properties of *Paradise Lost*, though he planned
his second epic with less expense of machines.
Nor is it probable that he read his *Paradise Lost*
as Shelley did, taking Satan as Prometheus in
opposition to the arbitrary Divine Right of
Heaven. But he felt that in *Paradise Lost* he
had wasted much of his strength. The two great
antagonists had never really faced one another,
and, in the absence of God the Father, Satan has
all the heroism to himself, that is, all the con-
tending strength, the athletic endurance and
speed. Milton felt this, and bent his mind
afresh to *Paradise Regained*. His motive was
not of course to satisfy Thomas Ellwood, or in
any way to confess, what would have been
obviously a ridiculous falsehood, that the scheme
of salvation had been left out of *Paradise Lost*.
His motive was to bring together, face to face
as combatants, the Adversary and the Redeemer ;
to represent a real debate, both parties keenly
engaged, instead of the indirect contention in
Paradise Lost, where the Antagonists occupy the
stage alternately. Hence the form of *Paradise
Regained*, which is unlike anything prescribed in
the ' Receipt to make an epic poem '. Milton has
broken away from the conventions of the critics

to invent a new form for himself, an epic which is mainly drama, a dialogue, a debate. The classical formal patterns have little to do with *Paradise Regained*.

I shall not stop to defend this poem against its detractors, nor to inquire whether there is too great a difference between the close-wrought speeches of the opponents and the more florid illustrations :

> Such forces met not, nor so wide a camp,
> When Agrican with all his northern powers
> Besieged Albracca, as romances tell,
> The city of Gallaphrone, from thence to win
> The fairest of her sex Angelica,
> His daughter, sought by many prowest knights,
> Both Paynim and the peers of Charlemain.

This quotation will be repeated some day in a lecture on Boiardo. It is strictly irrelevant here, except to show how dangerous Milton may be, leading the mind away into reminiscences of a vain amatorious poem.

Milton was not content with *Paradise Regained*. He had no reason to be dissatisfied with his characters. Unlike the antagonists of *Paradise Lost*, here Christ and Satan meet, and on seemingly fair terms. Each has his history ; and if Satan has no longer the magnitude of his former state, he is more subtle and complex ; a subject for Velazquez rather than for Michael Angelo. But the fault of the poem, Milton felt, was in the foregone conclusion. Satan has not a real chance ; we know that he must be defeated. Of course it may be said that all the old tragedies, and every tragedy when you see it for the second time, has a known conclusion. When we see Samson ' eyeless in Gaza at the mill with slaves ', we know that he will yet be revenged on the Philistines. Is not the other case the same, and the defeat of Satan simply a right ending to the story, which does not spoil the story, though it is known beforehand ? No, the difference is that there is always a chance for the Philistines ; they do really win some of their matches. Satan plays well ; but our knowledge that he is playing against Omnipotence, though Milton has done what he could to get over this, makes it impossible to work up the extreme tension which is required in tragedy. So Milton is driven on, beyond the epic dialogue of *Paradise Regained,* to the tragic form which of course had always been in his mind, along with all his other poetic learning. He writes his Greek tragedy because his thoughts have come to be perpetually bent on the tragic idea—not the external pattern of a blank verse drama with the unities preserved, and a chorus, but the living idea of an heroic soul under stress. In *Paradise Lost* and *Paradise Regained*, for one cause or another, the stress had slipped. ' Screw your courage to the sticking point ! ' Very well ; but the courage of Satan is flattened out, in both the stories, and the courage of Christ, in the second, never meets any strong ordeal, or any real choice between seemingly equal points of honour : there is nothing like the ordeal of Antigone, or of Neoptolemus in the *Philoctetes*. The success of *Paradise Regained*, considered as drama, is in the nearly equal dignity of the two opponents, the young Hero and the Prince of the Air. But much is lost when they come to the encounter ; Christ's Victory and Triumph is too easily won. Yet in *Paradise Regained* undoubtedly there is more appearance of an even contest than in *Paradise Lost*, and within the narrower limits the tide runs stronger. In *Samson* the channel is narrowed still more, and the mass of the flood goes through, full and strong—no large spaces like *Paradise Lost*, no bays and inlets as in *Paradise Regained*, but all one unhindered, unbroken force.

The drama of *Samson* is censured by Dr. Johnson (with reference to Aristotle's *Poetics*) because it has no middle. Dr. Johnson takes the different acts between the beginning and the end—particularly the scenes with Dalila and Harapha the giant—as simply episodes of conversation, 'nothing passes between the first act and the last that either hastens or delays the death of Samson'.

Crabb Robinson in his *Diary* tells how one day in 1829 he read *Samson Agonistes* to Goethe (following Byron's *Vision of Judgment*). Goethe made one remark, which I will repeat as it was told me by Professor Masson, who heard it from Crabb Robinson himself. Goethe said nothing till after ' Dalila his wife ' ; then he interrupted the reader and said : ' See the great poet ! he *putt* her in right ! '

Milton does not really mean to put Dalila in the right, but Goethe, with his sense of the stage, saw the theatrical value of Dalila which Dr. Johnson had failed to see. The action of the drama between the beginning and the end is the passion of Samson, beginning in the mood of affliction and remorse, turning more and more to hope and deliberate valour. The action is in the changes of mind leading on to the final victory ; these changes are not all of the same sort. Dalila, though ' a manifest serpent by her sting ', is

sufficiently in the right to provide some difficulties for Samson to refute if he can. One result
is that when Harapha of Gath comes in the next
act, Harapha is a relief. The giant is no trouble,
after Dalila, and Samson's vexation and anger in
the debate with his wife all turns to strength for
him in dealing with the Philistine champion.
His spirit has risen enormously ; that is the action
of the play. The great deliverer is now no longer
at the mill with slaves ; though he is blind he
is ready to fight Harapha :

Therefore without feigned shifts let be assigned
Some narrow place enclosed where sight may give thee,
Or rather flight, no great advantage on me ;
Then put on all thy gorgeous arms, thy helmet,
And brigandine of brass, thy broad habergeon,
Vant-brace and greaves and gauntlet ; add thy spear,
A weaver's beam, and seven-times-folded shield :
I only with an oaken staff will meet thee
And raise such outcries on thy clattered iron
Which long shall not withhold me from thy head
That in a little time while breath remains thee
Thou oft shalt wish thyself at Gath, to boast
Again in safety what thou wouldst have done
To Samson, but shalt never see Gath more.

(ll. 1116–29.)

In that way Samson goes on to the last exploit.
The scene with Harapha is necessary for the

action, and to save Samson from the mood of dejection in which he begins, and of recrimination in which the last scene has left him. Dalila his wife is so far in the right that Samson cannot be thoroughly in the right when he argues against her; he needs the plain question of courage to put him in possession of his strength; dealing with Harapha he knows where he is, and refuses to be blind.

I will not consider too curiously; I will read the last speech of Manoa and the last ode of the chorus in *Samson Agonistes*, a dramatic poem, the author John Milton :

Manoa. Come, come, no time for lamentation now,
   Nor much more cause, Samson hath quit himself
   Like Samson, and heroicly hath finish'd
   A life heroic, on his enemies
   Fully reveng'd, hath left them years of mourning,
   And lamentation to the Sons of Caphtor
   Through all Philistian bounds : to Israel
   Honour hath left, and freedom, let but them
   Find courage to lay hold on this occasion,
   To himself and Fathers house eternal fame ;
   And which is best and happiest yet, all this
   With God not parted from him, as was feard,
   But favouring and assisting to the end.
   Nothing is here for tears, nothing to wail
   Or knock the breast, no weakness, no contempt,

Dispraise, or blame, nothing but well and fair,
And what may quiet us in a death so noble.
Let us go find the body where it lies
Soak't in his enemies blood, and from the stream
With lavers pure and cleansing herbs wash off
The clotted gore. I with what speed the while
(Gaza is not in plight to say us nay)
Will send for all my kindred, all my friends
To fetch him hence and solemnly attend
With silent obsequie and funeral train
Home to his Fathers house : there will I build him
A monument, and plant it round with shade
Of Laurel ever green, and branching Palm,
With all his Trophies hung, and Acts enroll'd
In copious Legend, or sweet Lyric Song.
Thither shall all the valiant youth resort,
And from his memory inflame their breasts
To matchless valour, and adventures high :
The Virgins also shall on feastful days
Visit his Tomb with flowers, only bewailing
His lot unfortunate in nuptial choice,
From whence captivity and loss of eyes.
Chorus. All is best, though we oft doubt,
  What th' unsearchable dispose
  Of highest wisdom brings about,
  And ever best found in the close.
  Oft he seems to hide his face,
  But unexpectedly returns
  And to his faithful Champion hath in place
  Bore witness gloriously ; whence Gaza mourns
  And all that band them to resist

His uncontroulable intent,
His servants he with new acquist
Of true experience from this great event
With peace and consolation hath dismist,
And calm of mind all passion spent.

Samson in Milton's poem has long appeared
to me to have a likeness to another hero of
a different age and style : Roland, in the old
French epic. The likeness is this, that both
seem to stand for much more than themselves ;
for all the heroism in the world. Each has his
own character, but the character is more than
the man himself ; it is an idea, such that the
Song of Roland and his death in the pass of Ronce-
vaux may for some readers, by a kind of allegory,
though that is not the right word, represent
other stories, may be the poem of Gordon at
Khartoum, and of how many more ! Gaston
Paris lectured on Roland in 1871, when the
Prussians were at the gates : some of us listened
in London to Maurice Barrès when he took the
Chansons de Geste as the theme of his oration
on the spirit of France in the war. What the old
French epic wants in comparison with Homer
or Shakespeare it makes up in another way. We
do not think of Roland as we do of Achilles or
Odysseus. But Homer's men and Shakespeare's

are too strong in character to be anything but themselves ; the *Song of Roland* is more like music, in some respects, than drama ; so is *Samson Agonistes*. There is possibly a weakness in Handel's *Samson* : it is music for what is musical already ; the whole poem is musical, and the conclusion which I have just read is an heroic symphony.

Nothing is more difficult in art criticism than the problems taken up by Sir Joshua Reynolds in his discourses on the Grand Style. His definition of Ideal Beauty in paintings has been censured severely ; and what he says is open to the objections of Blake and Hazlitt—he gives too much the impression that ideal dignity is gained by abstraction, by leaving out what is characteristic and particular. Now Milton's Samson may help to explain what Blake meant when he insisted that great ideal figures are not abstract. The subject is too difficult, and I will leave it, only saying further that the objections to Reynolds's theory are probably for the most part objections to his language only, and not to his real meaning. I will add this, that Milton's last poem throws a reflection back to his earliest, the *Hymn for the Morning of Christ's Nativity*. The song of triumph over the rout of the old gods of the nations—

> Peor and Baalim
> Forsake their temples dim
> With that twice-batter'd god of Palestine—

that triumph is repeated in another mood forty years later, and the earlier poem, if you look back to it, takes fresh light from the victory of Samson.

ROMANTIC FALLACIES

THE title is not quite accurate: the fallacies of which I am to speak are not in Romance itself so much as in those who talk about it. 'Romance' is a dangerous word, and it is time that certain technical misuses of the name 'romantic' should be discouraged.

Mr. William Gilpin in his very pleasant Scotch tour [1] points out what he regards as a popular error in the indiscriminate use of the word 'picturesque' when what is really meant is 'romantic':

'On the right of the Pentland hills arises Arthur's seat: a rock which hangs over Edinburgh of peculiar appearance, romantic but not picturesque.' (i, p. 53.)

'A nearer approach did not give us a more pleasing idea of the environs of Edinburgh. We had always heard it represented as one of the most picturesque towns in Britain; but people often consider *romantic* and *picturesque* as synonyms. Arthur's seat, which is still the principal object, appears still as odd, misshapen and uncouth as before. . . . The town and castle indeed on the left make some amends, and are happily introduced.' (i, p. 59.)

[1] Observations relative chiefly to picturesque beauty, made in the year 1776, on several parts of Great Britain, particularly the Highlands of Scotland. (Published 1789.)

He does not explain what he means by ' romantic ',
but we can guess from his example. There must
be something strange or curious hindering or
thwarting the lines of pure harmonious beauty.

Sydney Smith perhaps may supply an example
of the confusion indicated by Gilpin. Sir Walter
Scott quotes an illustration from Sydney Smith's
famous lectures on Moral Philosophy at the Royal
Institution. To show the difference between the
Beautiful and the Picturesque he gave his audience
this : ' the Rector's horse is beautiful; the Curate's
is picturesque '. If he had studied Gilpin more
carefully, he would have said romantic.

It may be worth noticing here, whether it is
relevant or not, that Gilpin gives the highest
praise to the landscape that Scott loved as well
as any in the world, the view of the Tweed from
Fernielee, and that his pure taste in pictures is
not so strict and pedantic as to refuse acknow-
ledgement of what is added to the spirit of landscape by the charm of associations. He is in
a land of romance, by the fabled flood, and he
knows the power of songs to quicken the eye.
But he does not use the word romantic where
we should think it fitting enough : he has another
meaning, another use for it. Gilpin will be mentioned again, but for the present I leave him, and
come to part of the main business of this discourse.

I would ask whether the Romantic revival and the Romantic age of poetry have not been over-worked by critics and historians.

The Romantic Movement in English Poetry is the title of a book by Mr. Arthur Symons which ought to be better known, a book in which a poet reviews and judges all the poets of the great age, including many minor names, such as William Gifford and Robert Pollok, which are not there for praise. Now in this most lively and significant work, after the introduction, the idea of Romantic movement scarcely shows itself at all ; and the preface deals summarily with it, thus :

> ' The word " romantic " I think defines more clearly than any other what we find most characteristic in the renewal of poetry after its long banishment. The great poets of every age but the 18th have been romantic : what are Chaucer, Shakespeare and Coleridge if not romantic? '

Again, in the introduction :

> ' What is really meant by all these phrases and by the name of the romantic movement is simply the reawakening of the imagination, a reawakening to a sense of beauty and strangeness in natural things, and in all the impulses of the mind and the senses.'

If this is what romantic movement means, what are we to do as historians or critics when we come to inquire about things or poems that are indeed romantic ? For the sake of the language and the dictionary, ought we not to make a stand, and say that romance has meanings of its own, that ' romantic ' is too narrow a term for Chaucer and Shakespeare and a sense of beauty and strangeness in natural things and in all the impulses of the mind and the senses ?

We may note that ' classic ' and ' romantic ' are found together in Thomas Warton on Dante, ' this wonderful compound of classical and romantic fancy '.

Byron observes that people are beginning to speak of classic and romantic as opposites, and he read the early version of Stendhal's essay on Racine and Shakespeare, which is the programme of the great French contest between the old and the new school of drama.

The French romantics of the 1820's took their name from the German romantic school of a generation earlier. The Germans began the mischief, though they are not to blame for our mistaken adoption of their label.

In Germany first and then in France, ' romantic school ' had a definite meaning and justification, such as ' romantic revival ' has not in this country. The romantic school of the Schlegels, of Jean Paul Richter, Tieck, and the rest, for whom Carlyle worked so hard to get them accepted in England, was a natural product of Germany, where all literature was founded on criticism and self-conscious following of some or another model or ideal. German literature after its old glory in the time of the Minnesingers had fallen away behind the rest of Christendom ; it missed the Italian and the French renaissance, Petrarch, Ariosto, and Ronsard, and when it started again in the seventeenth century it had to learn its art of verse from the Netherlands and everything possible from France. Its greatest masters, Lessing and Goethe, are critics and theorists. The romantic school meant a new theory, a new policy, following on many older. But in England, where momentous and fertile imitations and adaptations had been accomplished in the sixteenth century by Wyatt and Surrey, Spenser and Marlowe, where so many forms of art had become traditional, there was no call for a romantic school—a self-conscious militant group —at the beginning of the nineteenth century, and *romantic* is a very partial and not very significant name for what really happened in the great revival of imagination.

Likewise in France in the day of *Hernani*, which Byron did not live to see, the factions classical and romantic had a meaning unlike anything that those badges could denote in England. The contest, as we know from the Memoirs of Alexandre Dumas and other historians, was an actual battle for the theatres. In England who are there to compare with the classical partisans of the old style of drama in France ? Byron counts up the names of those who are to be trusted to maintain the right :

'The disciples of Pope were Johnson, Goldsmith, Rogers, Campbell, Crabbe, Gifford, Mathias, Hayley, and the author of the *Paradise of Coquettes*, to whom may be added Richards, Heber, Wrangham, Bland, Hodgson, Merivale, and others who have not had their full fame. . . .'

As fighting men these are not to be compared with the French classical party, and there never was, and could not be, in England anything like the battle for which Victor Hugo gave his Spanish watchword *hierro* in 1830. If there was an English classical school, Byron was its principal advocate : one need say no more to show how different the conditions were in England and in France.

Romantic is a bad name for the poetry of the nineteenth century because it sets you looking for a common quality when you ought to be reading or remembering individual poems, and understanding the law of their being, to which end the romantic idea will not always help you much.

But romantic does mean something, and there was a romantic movement, which it might be interesting to trace and follow from its beginnings in the seventeenth century. Dryden gives it a name : ' the fairy way of writing ' ; Hurd names it : ' a world of fine fabling '. You can see it in the twin towers of All Souls, early eighteenth-century romantic art. Compare the towers with the outside of the Library : that also is eighteenth-century Gothic, but that is not romantic, like the towers. The library, outside, is sober imitation of the fifteenth century in the chapel opposite, not much exaggerating nor attempting any new effect. The towers are a romantic dream : look and see how the proportions of the windows are drawn out, intended to be sublime. Then go and look at the Library inside, that most perfect work of true and sound imagination in the eighteenth century. The towers are of the same date, but their romantic spirit is not allowed to distract the artist when he sees his way to nobler rhythms and harmonies.

Oxford, if not the original home of the romantic movement, has at any rate contributed largely, and was early in giving its help. Not only by its refusal to break absolutely with the Gothic tradition in architecture, but in literature also it showed the way to get new corn out of old fields.

' Romantic ' implies reminiscence : it means at first the sort of thing that is found in books of chivalry, or in the *Arcadia*, or in the *Grand Cyrus*. Hence the romantic schools have always depended more or less on the past ; their life is in

> beauty, making beautiful old rhyme,
> In praise of ladies dead and lovely knights.

It is a commonplace of literary history that between 1760 and 1770 Percy's *Reliques* and Macpherson's *Ossian* and Chatterton's *Rowley Poems* made all the difference. But it is not generally remembered that reliques of ancient poetry began to be studied, and were made available for the reading public and all youthful poets, long before.

In the philological series of the Clarendon Press there is no more entertaining and spirited work than the edition of *Christ's Kirk on the Green*, brought out by E. G. in 1691.

Edmund Gibson of Queen's was then not yet Bishop of London, but he had begun the studies which led later to his edition of the Saxon Chronicle, and with the help of the Press and all its founts he was able to publish this specimen of Scottish poetry :

> In Scotland was there never seen
> Sic dancing and deray,
> Neither at Falkland on the Green
> Nor Peebles to the play.

The commentary, which is the work of a scholar, is made as imposing as possible with Gothic, Anglo-Saxon, and Icelandic, each in its appropriate type, including, if I am not mistaken, one fount which Franciscus Junius had brought back from Sweden and presented to the University.

The same founts are used in a much larger work which was preparing at the same time, Hickes's *Thesaurus*, in three large volumes, containing everything wanted for a foundation in Germanic philology. In this vast medley Hickes included, immediately after the Anglo-Saxon poem of the *Fight at Finnesburh*, the Icelandic poem of the *Sword of Angantyr* : Hervor at her father's grave calling upon him to give her the sword Tyrfing, the invincible, the accursed sword. The mystery and terror of a haunted twilight, between the worlds of life and death, that is what the poem is, and something more ; the stress of human wills and passions, a high spirit of honour. There is nothing finer, in its way. And it was not left to philologers in the folio volume of Hickes's *Thesaurus*. By some unexplained and very amazing chance, this piece of Germanic philology was excerpted roughly and bodily out of the *Thesaurus*, and printed in one of the volumes of a new and amplified edition of Dryden's *Poetical Miscellany*. Percy translated

the poem later, and Lewis made use of it for
a tale of wonder, and the Sword of Angantyr is
one of the *Poèmes barbares* of Leconte de Lisle.
And, as I have said, it was a philological publication of this University which first discovered this
magic song more than 200 years ago.

I will not say much about the mediaeval studies
of Thomas Warton ; what he did for history and
scholarship and a fresh understanding of the
Middle Ages, and of Spenser and Milton as well,
is now continually more and more appreciated.
He owed much to his father, Thomas Warton
the elder, his ancestor in the chair of Poetry ;
something doubtless to his brother Joseph, who,
with less taste for exploration in old romance,
had a more secure and original judgement in
modern poetry. With Thomas Warton the
romantic revival or movement, or whatever it be
called, is well on its way, and it is recognized
by Dr. Johnson as something of a danger and
a provocation :

> Wheresoe'er I turn my view
> All is strange, yet nothing new,
> Endless labour all day long,
> Endless labour to be wrong,
> Phrase that time has flung away,
> Uncouth words in disarray,
> Trick'd in antique ruff and bonnet,
> Ode and elegy and sonnet.

Johnson was provoked at Warton's excesses in old English poetry. Warton and Johnson were friends all the same, and we may digress here to think of them on the road home to Oxford from Elsfield, Warton quickening too much for Johnson, and Johnson calling out ' *sufflamina* ' (put on your brake chain).

There is nothing in mediaeval philology that is essentially dangerous to a classical mind. The most absurd and pedantic railer at Shakespeare, the determined advocate of the dramatic unities, Thomas Rymer, was one of the pioneers, for England, in the old poetry of Provence. It would have been well, anyhow it would have been pleasant, if he had had more followers and earlier, to discover what beauty there is in the Provençal lyric, from which all modern verse is derived, to perceive how little the poetry of Bernart de Ventadorn needs any allowance on the score of time or circumstance ; with what pride and confidence the Provençal poets may claim to have their work tested by as severe a standard as you please.

This really is where the romantic fallacy, or a fallacy about romance, has done most harm. Once the contrast of classical and romantic has been imposed on the mind, the reader of mediaeval verse thinks romantically, and sees his authors

quaintly doing quaint things in old-fashioned
rhyme. It would not be difficult to find two or
three Provençal lyrics of the twelfth century perfect in rhythm and measure under the same rules
of art as Gray or Wordsworth, complete and
rounded also in their poetical argument. A truer
sense of classical poetry and some further study
of the Middle Ages might have brought out the
classical quality of Provençal and German lyric
ages before Dante and Petrarch.

Addison on *Chevy Chase* is a very striking
example of what might have been done with more
research in olden treasures of poetry. When we
talk of romantic revival, let us remember *Chevy
Chase*, and how Addison read and praised the old
ballad for its classic quality, its sincerity, its sense
of proportion, how he used the old ballad to
threaten and cow our little Gothic artists, the
trifling conceited poets of his day. Dryden,
twelve years earlier, in the Preface to the *Fables*,
had given another example of the same sort of
independent judgement, when he praised Chaucer
for his truth of imagination, and blamed Ovid for
his trifling ornament.

There was a romantic movement, then, which
began before the eighteenth century, and it can
be traced, and it is not altogether dull work
tracing it. It does not come all from philology,

or all from the Middle Ages—some of it comes from the Hebrides, and a man from Sussex writes an ode on the *Superstitions of the Highlands*. The Hebrides always tell in poetry : there was a happy false reading of their name : strictly they ought to be ' Ebudes ', but ' Ebudes ' will not do in poetry, any more than ' Ioua insula ', which is the true Latin for Icolmcille, can compete in verse or prose with ' Iona '.

Milton began in *Lycidas* :

> Whether beyond the stormy Hebrides,
> Where thou perhaps under the whelming tide
> Visit'st the bottom of the monstrous world.

Thomson took it up in the *Castle of Indolence*, the most purely romantic poem before the *Ancient Mariner* :

> Or as some shepherd of the Hebrid isles,
> Placed far amid the melancholy main.

And Collins comes after with his *Ode*. It might have been well if more had been learned for modern fancy-work from Skye or Jura ; the fairy mythology of the Western Islands is not false, like much of the conventional literary fairy tales. Shakespeare is responsible, through Drayton and Herrick, for much artificial prettiness in a kingdom of Oberon utterly different from the sombre, splendid region, underground, within the hill.

Thomson in the *Castle of Indolence* and Collins in his *Ode* escape the literary convention of pert tripping fairies and dapper elves. Collins is not always safe : in his finest poem there are elves who sleep in flowers the day.

Nothing is more significant for the progress of the romantic movement and its danger, and the escape of true poetic imagination from the danger, than the stanza which Collins struck out, and the stanza that took its place in the second version of the *Ode to Evening* :

1747.

> Then let me rove some wild and heathy scene,
> Or find some ruin midst its dreary dells,
>> Whose walls more awful nod
>> By thy religious gleams.

1748 (Dodsley).

> Then lead, calm votaress, where some sheety lake
> Cheers the lone heath, or some time-hallowed pile,
>> Or upland fallows grey
>> Reflect its last cool gleam.

In the second version, besides the true personification in ' votaress ', who is from Milton's *Maske*, there is the fresh vision and understanding of the effect of a surface of water in twilight, when all the land round it is dark, and in place of the conventional ruin that ' nods ', there is the old building, church or castle, dimly seen as part of the evening light along with the large bulging hillside. If you look into it, you will see at once that the water is to the west, the ' time-hallowed pile ' to the east, and all this is given in the fewest words, and with no vanity or insistence on the accurate rendering. The romantic fallacy is cleared away, and its place is taken in a different mode of vision and of poetry.

The progress of poetry in the eighteenth century, as later, as now, is not controlled by influences or fashions that can be called either romantic or the opposite. Romantic or classical may denote fashions of the reading public or of pedantic criticism, but the hope of poetry is simply in new minds free to choose their own way. The comparative blankness of the eighteenth century, the richness of the new age that followed, was not due to fashion or programme. All the difference was made by the birth of two or three infants in the early seventies, Wordsworth, Scott, and Coleridge, and a few more a little later, Byron, Shelley, and Keats. Their success did not come from a general tide of thought—their wits would have succeeded whatever the fashion of the time might be. ' Romantic revival ' and other such terms are well enough for the general history of culture, ' typical developments '; but such terms may prevent you from understanding what

William Wordsworth was thinking when he wrote
the *Ode to Duty*, or the *Poem on Rob Roy's Grave*,
what possessed the mind of Shelley to bring out
his tragedy of *The Cenci*.

One of our own poets in this College, a
quondam Fellow, Dr. Edward Young, not very
thoroughly successful himself as a poet, was able
at the age of seventy-five to write a piece of good
advice to young adventurers in poetry, an essay
rather glorious in its style, and I think sound in
its judgement, a letter to the author of *Sir Charles
Grandison*, in 1759, which really adds something
more to that wonderful year—the year of Quebec
and Minden and so many other victories, also of
Goldsmith's tract on the *Present State of Polite
Learning in Europe*, a gloomy prospect of blight
and decay.

Young had written a poem on *The Last Day*
more absurd in places than any other composition
on that dangerous theme : Satires, which were
only not good enough to compete with Pope.
Zanga in the *Revenge* long held the stage and
deserved all he got : a most dexterous adaptation
of Iago to a plot more simple and for certain
purposes more telling than Shakespeare's ; nearer
the concentrated effect of Victor Hugo. Then
the *Night Thoughts* ; the work of a man growing
old, still ready for new experiments, and carrying

this well through, in a fresh sort of blank verse, not that of the eighteenth-century Miltonic tradition, not like Thomson's *Seasons*, but drier, keener ; and, for matter, discoursing on life and death with a more personal touch than was common. Young's letter on original composition is not meant to help any active project of his own. It is a free survey of the state of poetry, and a call for fresh and original work, for narrative poetry not delayed with ornament, for tragedy with a heart in it. A very remarkable thing, as was said at the time, to have been written by an old man.

Young does not give any particular prescription how the thing is to be done, except that he finds fault with Pope's use of rhyme for epic : a curious point when it is compared with Goldsmith's perpetual hatred of blank verse, first stated in his tract of this same year, where he finds English poetry far gone in decrepitude : ' the affected security of our odes, the tuneless flow of our blank verse '.

Young simply says, do not imitate ; be original ; be individual. Young is hard on Dryden, but what he says may be edifying apart from the question of Dryden's fame :

' Dryden had a great but a general capacity ; and as for a general genius, there is no such thing in nature.

A genius implies the rays of the mind concenter'd, and determined to some particular point ; when they are scattered widely, they act feebly, and strike not with sufficient force to fire, or dissolve, the heart.'

I take this, and the whole of Young's *Conjectures on Original Composition*, as a denial and refusal of any programme, prescription, rule, school, faction, influence, or agency, except what may be found or chosen by the poet himself when he bends his mind to his work. One thing I would note particularly, one reason for his hopeful spirit. Writing to the author of *Sir Charles Grandison*, he tells him that :

' A friend of mine has obeyed that injunction [to make original use of his talent] and with a genius as well *moral* as *original* (to speak in bold terms) has cast out evil spirits ; has made a convert to virtue of a species of composition once most its foe.'

His friend Mr. Richardson has reclaimed the novel, and we may allow some credit to the spirit of the age for that event : the novelists had given a good example to the poets ; they had shown them, as the old song says, ' there 's gear to win ye never saw '. And the new age came : Young was writing in the year that Burns was born.

By making too much of the name ' romantic ' the critics and historians have troubled the study of poetry in two ways. They have made it harder to seize what was airy and evanescent already, those strange flowers of poetry that seem to live almost without any ground or substance, especially in the ballads. What am I thinking of ? Such things as the ballad refrains ' by the bonny mill-dams o' Binnorie ', and in the cruel story of the robbers :

> He has killed this maid and has laid her by,
> For to bear the red rose company.

I am thinking of the Spanish ballad of the Count Arnaldos, and the mariner's song from the strange galley; and the Icelandic ballad of Tristram :

> Isolt goes from the sea inland,
>   The street was long,
> And ever she heard the bells ringing
>   The goodly song.
>
> Isolt went from the sea inland,
>   The way was straight,
> And ever she heard the bells ringing
>   As she came thereat.
>
> Then she spake, the fair Isolt,
>   From over the foam,
> Nay, but Tristram should not die
>   When I come home.
>
> Out on the floor the priests were standing
>   With tapers fair,
> Queen Isolt came where Tristram lay,
>   And knelt there.

To many a man in the world is given
    Sorrow and pain,
The Queen knelt down and died there, Isolt,
    Where he lay slain.

Out on the floor the priests they stood,
    Their dirges said,
The bells of gold were rung for Isolt
    And Tristram dead.

(*Nothing for them was shapen but to sunder.*)

I think also of many things in Greek and Latin poetry, of Pindar's vision, East of the Sun, West of the Moon ; of Milanion in Propertius, a love-lorn wanderer among the rocks of Arcadia. There is no end, fortunately, to those recollections, though no more need be said about them now.

POPE

FOR many years past, ever since the publication of Joseph Warton's *Essay on the Writings and Genius of Pope*, the poetry of Pope has been judged indirectly and with deference to opinions, cavils, and misgivings about him; even Dr. Johnson does not ignore ' the question that has been put ', whether Pope is a poet. Warton's Essay, the controversies of Bowles and Byron, are apt to come between the reader and his author. Pope is valued not exactly as he is, but as he is thought about. He is judged through ' second intentions ': a phrase which in another place than this might appear to be pedantic, but in Oxford, the proper home and seat of Queen Entelechy and the old logic of the schools, to speak of ' second intentions ' is surely allowable :

—still
Doth the old instinct bring back the old names!

The estimate of Pope's poetry, more than of any other poet, is made through the judgement of other people. Swinburne is one of the few who disregard the stale problem; in his essay on Dryden and Pope (disguised under the title *A Century of English Poetry*) he goes on proudly

and happily, enjoying and praising, in spite of
the temptation to touch on Matthew Arnold,
who makes Dryden and Pope into ' classics of
our prose ', or on Mark Pattison, whose sentence
is that ' Pope had no thought, no mind, no ideas,
but he had the art of rhymed language in a degree
in which no English poet before or since has
possessed it '. But let us leave *secundas inten-
tiones in vacuo* to the chimera whose food they
probably are. Let the authors speak. And this
is what you hear (for example) from the author
of *Absalom and Achitophel* :

> The Jews, a headstrong moody murm'ring race
> As ever tried the extent and stretch of grace,
> God's pamper'd people whom debauch'd with ease
> No king could govern nor no God could please :
> (Gods they had tried of ev'ry shape and size
> That godsmiths could produce or priests devise)
> And when no rule, no precedent was found
> Of men by laws less circumscrib'd and bound,
> They led their wild desires to rocks and caves,
> And thought that all but savages were slaves.

Is there anything equal to that in Pope, the
pupil of Dryden, the master of rhymed language ?
What shall we try ?

> The skilful Nymph reviews her force with care :
> Let spades be trumps, she said, and trumps they were.
> Now move to war her sable Matadores,
> In show like leaders of the swarthy Moors.

Spadillio first, unconquerable Lord!
Led off two captive trumps and swept the board.
As many more *Manillio* forced to yield
And march'd a victor from the verdant field.
Him *Basto* followed, but his fate more hard
Gain'd but one trump and one Plebeian card.
With his broad sabre next, a chief in years,
The hoary Majesty of Spades appears,
Puts forth one manly leg, to sight reveal'd;
The rest his many colour'd robe conceal'd.
The rebel Knave who dares his prince engage,
Proves the just victim of his royal rage;
Ev'n mighty *Pam*, that Kings and Queens o'erthrew
And mow'd down armies in the fights of Lu,
Sad chance of war! now destitute of aid
Falls undistinguish'd by the victor spade!

Who doubts that the *Rape of the Lock* is Pope's most perfect work? It is one of the few things wholly without a flaw: is it vain and futile to ask where the music comes from and what it is worth with all its perfection?

It is not easy to understand without some pieces of ancient learning. There is pedantry in it, or what seems so to us who do not take the Heroic Poem as seriously as Milton, Dryden, and Pope; and unless you think seriously about the Epic, the Heroic Poem, you cannot think rightly of the *Rape of the Lock*, an Heroi-Comical Poem. This descriptive epithet is part of the tradition: it is used by Tassoni and Boileau. Pope was

haunted by the orthodox critical doctrine of the
Epic Poem. Like Milton and Dryden, he had the
epic ambition; he wrote *Alcander Prince of
Rhodes* when he was a boy; he made the plan of
Brutus, an epic, when he was older. He saw the
absurdity of the formalists such as the Reverend
Father Le Bossu; he wrote for Steele's *Guardian*
the comic receipt to make an epic poem which
was incorporated in Martinus Scriblerus on the
Art of Sinking in Poetry. But his preface to
the *Iliad* goes over, seriously, the same divisions
of the subject: Fable, Characters, Machines,
Allegory. His plan of *Brutus* follows the
receipt; the fable is taken from Geoffrey of
Monmouth, the machines are guardian angels
of kingdoms, such as Dryden had recommended.
He puts the old allegories into his Homer. The
revised version of the *Rape of the Lock*, the very
successful ' machinery ' of sylphs and gnomes, is
something more than play; it is parody of one
of the most important things in life for Pope,
and his heroi-comical expedient, his most excellent
lively burlesque substitute for the Olympians of
Homer, is valued by him for its epic quality and
its faithfulness to the epic idea. Pope makes his
story out of no elements that are ungraceful; he
aims at beauty, and the *Rape of the Lock*, a poem
with no substance at all, is nothing but grace;

the astral body of an heroic poem, pure form, an echo of divine music, how thin and clear !

This heroi-comical poem, if it is his finest and most absolute work, still does not fully give all his range, all his power : and Pope himself did not reckon it as letting him off the task of true heroic poetry. He went on to Homer ; the first volume published in 1715 gives his opinion in the Preface : fifteen years after Dryden's Preface to his Fables and no less remarkable for its freedom of speech and its unlikeness to the poetry which it precedes. Both Dryden and Pope in their prose say things which their verse cannot say, and declare themselves, express themselves, more freely. Dryden's comparison of Chaucer and Ovid tells you more of Dryden's mind and temper than his paraphrase of the Knight's Tale ; Pope's description of Homer tells you something of Pope which you do not find explicitly in his verse. Here let me say with the greatest respect for Matthew Arnold that his description of Dryden and Pope as ' classics of our prose ' is a double sin in criticism, because it confuses the kinds in two ways ; ignoring their poetry and their prose alike. For of course they are classics of our prose, when they write prose. Pope as a prose writer comes between Dryden and Johnson, less large in his periods than the older man, less formal

than the younger. All three have the same
strength of admiration, the same glorious delight
when they meet with great poets. And this is
Pope's theory of Homer :

' It is to the strength of this amazing invention we
are to attribute that unequalled fire and rapture which
is so forcible in Homer that no man of a true poetical
spirit is master of himself while he reads him. What
he writes is of the most animated nature imaginable ;
everything moves, everything lives and is put in action.
If a council be called or a battle fought, you are not
coldly informed of what was said or done as from
a third person ; the reader is hurried out of himself
by the force of the poet's imagination, and turns in
one place to a hearer, in another to a spectator. The
course of his verses resembles that of the army he
describes

οἱ δ᾽ ἄρ᾽ ἴσαν, ὡσεί τε πυρὶ χθὼν πᾶσα νέμοιτο.

They pour along like a fire that sweeps the whole
earth before it. It is however remarkable that his
fancy, which is everywhere vigourous, is not discovered
immediately at the beginning of his poem in its fullest
splendour ; it grows in the progress, both upon himself and others, and becomes on fire like a chariot wheel
by its own rapidity. Exact disposition, just thought,
correct elocution, polished numbers, may have been
found in a thousand, but this poetical fire, this *vivida
vis animi,* in a very few. Even in works where all
those are imperfect or neglected, this can overpower
criticism and make us admire even while we dis-
approve. Nay, where this appears, though attended

with absurdities, it brightens all the rubbish about it, till we see nothing but its own splendour. This *fire* is discerned in Virgil, but discerned as through a glass, reflected from Homer, more shining than fierce, but everywhere equal and constant : in Lucan and Statius it bursts out in sudden short and interrupted flashes : in Milton it glows like a furnace kept up to an uncommon ardour by the force of art : in Shakespeare it strikes before we are aware, like an accidental fire from heaven : but in Homer, and in him only, it burns everywhere clearly, and everywhere·irresistibly.'

Fire is Pope's element : Pope returns to ' the *fire* of the poem ' later in the same preface : this is what he says of Chapman : ' that which is to be allowed him, and which very much contributed to cover his defects, is a daring fiery spirit that animates his translation, which is something like what we might imagine Homer himself would have writ before he arrived to years of discretion '. Of course Pope believed that he himself possessed a daring fiery spirit ; and, that being so, his ideal of verse ought not to be an ideal of glaze and polish, ' fix'd as in a frost ' ; his ideal of verse is not very different from Dryden's. Is his practice different ? It is not exactly the same, certainly. An essay by an old friend of mine, Mr. Armine Kent of Balliol, on the *Crime of Alexander Pope*, shows what is implied in Cowper's complaint that Pope's musical finesse had made poetry a mechanic art for his imitators. Kent was a great admirer of Pope, and his charge is delivered only against the mechanical warblers who copied him. Did Pope himself in his own practice spoil the old heroic couplet and make it too complete, too separate, too epigrammatic ? We may answer this by saying that Pope had many different aims and varieties of style. He certainly knew how to work in mosaic, and Swift describes him so engaged :

> Each atom by another struck
> All shapes and motions tries,
> Till in a lump together stuck
> Behold a poem rise.

Sometimes it pleased him to put together independent couplets and make a string of pointed sentences out of them ; but nevertheless his fiery spirit would not allow great arguments to be broken up into separate verses and couplets ; and in fact he carries on long periods with nearly the same success as Dryden—does not that come out in Belinda's game ?—is not that a well-sustained heroic battle ? While on the other hand Dryden's strength and eloquence carry with them the same talent for epigram as Pope's. Dryden's brilliance in this respect is not denied by any one ; what is less generally recognized

is Pope's power of keeping up an argument or
a story so that it grows in effect and overrides
the single couplets. Neither Dryden nor Pope
has always the same wave length ; both of them
are sometimes choppy, and in both of them you
often find the short waves carried on the back
of a long swell.

Pope in his *Iliad* took some trouble to escape
monotony. He has calendared his experiments
in the *Poetical Index* under the head ' Versification expressing in the sound the thing describ'd '.
The interest of this Index and those passages is
of course that they show how seriously Pope
believed in his own teaching about the sound and
the sense, in the *Essay on Criticism*. They also
show how he could break the traditional rules of
the couplet in order to carry on his story. The
regular couplet had been no sooner fixed than it
was challenged. Prior in his *Solomon* claimed the
freedom of running on the sense : Pope says
nothing about this, as Prior does, in his preface,
but his verse can be remarkably unlike the
ordinary fashion. Here is a quotation from the
twenty-third Book of the *Iliad*—a passage which
is noted in the Index for three imitations : ' the
rattling and jumping of carts over a rough and
rocky way ', ' a sudden fall ', and ' the rattling and
crashing of trees falling '.

Thus while he spoke, each Eye grew big with Tears :
And now the rosy-finger'd Morn appears,
Shews every mournful Face with Tears o'erspread,
And glares on the pale Visage of the Dead.
But *Agamemnon*, as the Rites demand,
With Mules and Waggons sends a chosen Band ;
To load the Timber and the Pile to rear,
A Charge consign'd to Merion's faithful Care.
With proper Instruments they take the Road,
Axes to cut, and Ropes to sling the Load.
First march the heavy Mules, securely slow,
O'er Hills, o'er Dales, o'er Crags, o'er Rocks, they go :
Jumping high o'er the Shrubs of the rough Ground,
Rattle the clatt'ring bars, and the shockt Axles bound.
But when arriv'd at *Ida's* spreading Woods,
(Fair *Ida*, water'd with descending Floods)
Loud sounds the Axe, rebounding Strokes on Strokes ;
On all sides round the Forest hurles her Oaks
Headlong. Deep-echoing groan the Thickets brown ;
Then rustling, crackling, crashing, thunder down.
The Wood the *Grecians* cleave, prepar'd to burn ;
And the slow Mules the same rough Road return.

Now we see the meaning of that couplet
quoted by Spence from Pope's martyred epic
of *Alcander* :

> Shields, helms, and swords all jangle as they hang
> And sound formidinous with angry clang.

Why did Atterbury allow or advise Pope to burn
Alcander ? It must have been a spirited story :
if it was not otherwise like *Endymion*, at any rate

it had, like *Endymion*, an under-sea adventure ;
the swords that jangle as they hang are portents
of romance. Shall we mourn for *Alcander* ?
At any rate Alcander Prince of Rhodes has
escaped the danger of a dissertation, and the
schools have lost a subject : they are not expected
to *Compare Pope and Keats in a submarine light,
and allude to Beowulf in this connexion.* Is it
fanciful to think that the sea, of which he knew
little or nothing, had great power over the mind
of Pope ?

> He steer'd securely and discover'd far
> Led by the light of the Maeonian star.

Aristotle is thought of as a voyager. Brutus in
the story as Pope had sketched it puts out, like
Dante's Ulysses, through the Pillars of Hercules
to the Atlantic ; he sails to Norway and the
Orkneys, and probably to Iceland, before he
undertakes the settlement of Britain. I return to
Pope's Homer.

Coleridge speaks of Pope's Homer as the chief
ource of the conventional pseudo-poetic diction
which drew Wordsworth's attack. Coleridge,
the inventor of ' pantisocracy ' and ' esemplastic ',
author of ' defecates to a pure transparency ', is
not unfair to Pope's original work ; on the
contrary he recognizes and praises the excellence
and ease of his style when he is writing for him-

self. He is probably unjust to Pope's Homer.
Sir Walter Raleigh makes Milton the chief
model of pseudo-poetic diction : and Pope would
not disagree with this ; in his postscript to the
Odyssey he speaks of the imitators of Milton and
how they overdo their archaism. This essay of
Pope's is worth reading if only as an answer to
Wordsworth and Coleridge : it says clearly what
Wordsworth was always more or less meaning
to say in his argument about the language of
poetry. Pope himself thought well of this essay ;
better, he said, than the preface to the *Iliad*,
where he was too much on the high horse. It
gives a true reading of the *Odyssey* as including
everything in human life ; it gives a fine description of the poet's style and language as they
change with the mood and matter of the story and
the dialogue. The *Odyssey* is not for him a stiff
formal classical composition : it is as various as
Shakespeare.

' There is a real beauty in an easy, pure, perspicuous
description even of a *low action*. There are numerous
instances of this both in *Homer* and *Virgil* ; and perhaps those natural passages are not the least pleasing
of their works. It is often the same in History, where
the representations of common, or even domestic
things, in clear, plain, and natural words, are frequently
found to make the liveliest impression on the reader.

' The question is, how far a Poet, in pursuing the

description or image of an action, can attach himself to *little circumstances*, without vulgarity or trifling? what particulars are proper, and enliven the image; or what are impertinent, and clog it? In this matter Painting is to be consulted, and the whole regard had to those circumstances which contribute to form a full, and yet not a confused, idea of a thing.'

' *Homer* in his lowest narrations or speeches is ever easy, flowing, copious, clear, and harmonious. He shows not less *invention*, in assembling the humbler, than the greater, thoughts and images; nor less *judgment*, in proportioning the style and the versification to these than to the other. Let it be remember'd, that the same Genius that soar'd the highest, and from whom the greatest models of the *Sublime* are derived, was also he who stoop'd the lowest, and gave to the simple *Narrative* its utmost perfection. Which of these was the harder task to *Homer* himself, I cannot pretend to determine; but to his Translator I can affirm (however unequal all his imitations must be) that of the latter has been much the more difficult.

' Whoever expects here the same pomp of verse, and the same ornaments of diction, as in the Iliad; he will, and he ought to be disappointed. Were the original otherwise, it had been an offence against nature; and were the translation so, it were an offence against *Homer*, which is the same thing.'

' Some use has been made to this end, of the style of *Milton*. A just and moderate mixture of old words may have an effect like the working old Abbey stones into a building, which I have sometimes seen to give a kind of venerable air, and yet not destroy the neat-

ness, elegance, and equality requisite to a new work;
I mean without rendring it too unfamiliar, or remote
from the present purity of writing, or from that ease
and smoothness which ought always to accompany
Narration or Dialogue. In reading a style judiciously
antiquated, one finds a pleasure not unlike that of
travelling on an old *Roman* way; but then the road
must be as *good*, as the way is *antient*; the style must
be such in which we may evenly proceed, without
being put to short stops by sudden abruptnesses, or
puzled by frequent turnings and transpositions: No
Man delights in furrows and stumbling-blocks: And
let our love to Antiquity be ever so great, a fine ruin
is one thing, and a heap of rubbish another. The
imitators of *Milton*, like most other imitators, are not
Copies but *Caricatura's* of their original; they are
a hundred times more obsolete and cramp than he,
and equally so in all places; Whereas it should have
been observed of *Milton*, that he is not lavish of his
exotick words and phrases every where alike, but
employs them much more where the subject is mar-
vellous vast and strange, as in the scenes of Heaven,
Hell, Chaos, &c. than where it is turned to the natural
and agreeable, as in the pictures of Paradise, the loves
of our first parents, the entertainments of Angels, and
the like. In general, this unusual style better serves
to awaken our ideas in the descriptions and in the
imaging and picturesque parts, than it agrees with
the lower sort of narrations, the character of which is
simplicity and purity. *Milton* has several of the latter,
where we find not an antiquated, affected, or uncouth
word, for some hundred lines together; as in his fifth

book, the latter part of the eighth, the former of the
tenth and eleventh books, and in the narration of
Michael in the twelfth. I wonder indeed that he,
who ventur'd (contrary to the practice of all other
Epic Poets) to imitate *Homer's* Lownesses in the *Narrative*, should not also have copied his plainness and
perspicuity in the *Dramatic* parts : Since in his speeches
(where clearness above all is necessary) there is frequently such transposition and forced construction,
that the very sense is not to be discovered without
a second or third reading : and in this certainly he
ought to be no example.'

Now what are Pope's original poems worth, if
they are not this same variety ? ' The narrow
sound of Satire ', if I may use a phrase and figure
of Swinburne's, opens out to a large sea; the
beauty of his satiric poetry is its reflection of
the whole world, not steadily or as the great
masters render it in Epic or Tragedy, but with
all the lights of the greater modes represented
here and there—so that anywhere you may
be caught away, for a moment, to different
regions.

The postscript to the *Odyssey* explains Pope's
ideal of poetic expression, and this is what he
actually obtains in his own poetry.

He is a master of point and epigram ; but this
is not what makes his success. Other writers
have done as well in separate pieces. There is

nothing better in one way than Prior's address
to Boileau :

> I grant, old friend, old foe (for such we are
> Alternate as the chance of peace and war)—

the very spirit of the old courtesy, so notable in
the wars and intervals of war through the
eighteenth century, here mingled with irony, but
not so as to detract from the grace of the gesture.

For satirical art in direct attack no one can do
much better than Johnson's imitation of Juvenal,
giving the London equivalent of the Roman poets
reciting in the Dog-days :

> Here falling houses thunder on your head,
> And here a female atheist talks you dead.

Or one might quote, for point and malice, that
single couplet of Gray on the ecclesiastical
history of Britain :

> When love had taught a monarch to be wise
> And gospel light first dawn'd from Bullen's eyes.

For another mood Tickell in his lament for
Addison—a poem honoured by Swift—has drawn
from the heroic couplet its deepest music :

> Never to mansions where the mighty rest
> Since their foundation came a nobler guest.

As deep as this and as solemn, Johnson on *The
Vanity of Human Wishes* :

> How few there are whom hours like these await
> Who set unclouded in the gulfs of Fate—

From Goldsmith, from Akenside's *Epistle to Curio*, from *The New Morality* in the *Anti-Jacobin*, it would be easy enough to quote single couplets that are not ' distained ' by any jewel of Pope's ; and Pope's superiority is not merely in his larger store of such things. The beauty of Pope's verse is its living variety ; the wave changes its colour, you might say, as the sun or the cloud takes it, as it runs green over the sands, or blue over the deep water. You never can be certain from the subject what the language and the tune will be like ; and the advantage of Satire, which is not the highest order of Poetry, is that it can at any moment take the reflection of epic or tragedy. The *Dunciad*, a mock heroic poem more villainous than any of the old ribald travesties of Homer or Virgil, ends in the way we know, beyond all praise

> Lo ! thy dread empire CHAOS is restor'd :
> Light dies before thy uncreating word :
> Thy hand, great Anarch, lets the curtain fall—

while before you come to this magnificence you find the couplet which Pope thought the most musical of all his verse :

> Lo ! where Maeotis sleeps, and hardly flows
> The freezing Tanais through a waste of snows.

It does not need the grand style to bring out the strength of Pope ; it is shown in a touch here and there, in the effect of a seemingly light and ordinary phrase:

> Like Journals, Odes, *and such forgotten things*
> As Eusden, Philips, Settle writ of Kings.

The phrase comes again in *Sordello*:

> To clear away with such forgotten things
> As are an eyesore to the morn,

and it may be through Browning's repetition that we notice it more readily in Pope.

The old device of *Alcander*, the ' angry clang ', reappears in the description of Blackmore:

> What! like Sir Richard, rumbling, rough and fierce,
> With ARMS and GEORGE and BRUNSWICK crowd the verse;
> Rend with tremendous sound your ears asunder
> With Gun, Drum, Trumpet, Blunderbuss and Thunder;
> Or nobly wild, with Budgel's fire and force,
> Paint Angels trembling round his falling horse.

A different sort of phrasing in the *Essay on Man*, Epistle IV, at the beginning. Before I read it may I say that I think the *Essay on Man* is too much neglected: taken as a curiosity, part of the history of English thought in the eighteenth century, an example of popular philosophy ' in the best of all possible worlds '. Some of it is difficult, the sentences, like the reasoning, clogged; some of it is too merely rhetorical:

> The lamb thy riot dooms to bleed to-day;

some of it is sinking in poetry :

> Why has not man a microscopic eye?
> For this plain reason, man is not a fly—

though this slip is pretty well recovered in what
follows. But the Essay contains some of the best
of Pope's poetry ; the passage on Fame, and
this, in a different way :

> Oh Happiness ! our being's end and aim !
> Good, Pleasure, Ease, Content, whate'er thy name,
> That something still which prompts the eternal sigh
> For which we bear to live, or dare to die,
> Which still so near us, yet beyond us lies,
> O'erlook'd, seen double, by the fool, and wise.
> Plant of celestial seed ! if dropt below
> Say in what mortal soil thou deign'st to grow :
> Fair op'ning to some Court's propitious shine,
> Or deep with di'monds in the flaming mine?
> Twin'd with the wreaths Parnassian laurels yield
> Or reap'd in iron harvests of the field?
> Where grows? where grows it not?

Something of Pope's style may be learned from
a reference to ' iron harvest ' as he had used the
phrase in his Statius :

> How with the serpent's teeth he sow'd the soil,
> And reap'd an iron harvest of his toil.

Here it is no more than a conceit ; the import,
the value, is different in the *Essay on Man*.

I will not quote the passage about his friends

in the *Epistle to Arbuthnot*, but I will ask you
to remember what Charles Lamb thought of it,
and how he read it at that evening party a hundred years ago which is described by Hazlitt in
the essay *Of Persons we would wish to have seen*,
which is, throughout, Hazlitt's truest recollection
of Charles Lamb, as the essay *My First Acquain-
tance with Poets* is nothing but Coleridge. But
I must repeat the opening of the *Epistle to
Arbuthnot*, for it has long appeared to me, if
not the best of Pope at any rate the most expressive of all his confessions.

> Shut, shut the door, good John ! fatigu'd I said :
> Tie up the knocker, say I'm sick, I'm dead.
> The Dog-star rages ! nay, 'tis past a doubt,
> All Bedlam, or Parnassus, is let out :
> Fire in each eye, and papers in each hand,
> They rave, recite, and madden round the land.
>   What walls can guard me, or what shades can hide?
> They pierce my thickets, thro' my grot they glide.
> By land, by water, they renew the charge ;
> They stop the chariot and they board the barge.
> No place is sacred, not the Church is free ;
> Ev'n Sunday shines no Sabbath-day to me.
> Then from the Mint walks forth the Man of rhyme,
> Happy to catch me, just at Dinner-time.
>   Is there a Parson, much bemus'd in beer,
> A maudlin Poetess, a rhyming Peer,
> A Clerk, foredoom'd his father's soul to cross
> Who pens a Stanza when he should *engross*?

Is there who lock'd from ink and paper scrawls
With desp'rate charcoal round his darken'd walls?
All fly to *Twit'nam*, and in humble strain
Apply to me, to keep them mad or vain.
Arthur, whose giddy son neglects the laws,
Imputes to me and my damn'd works the cause;
Poor *Cornus* sees his frantic wife elope,
And curses wit, and poetry, and Pope.

Nothing of Pope's poetry and not the whole of it all together represents fully what he thought and admired. Spenser was one of his favourite poets, all his life long; his praise of Shakespeare goes far beyond the limits of his own poetry.

' I will conclude by saying of *Shakespear*, that with all his faults, and with all the irregularity of his *Drama*, one may look upon his works, in comparison of those that are more finish'd and regular, as upon an ancient majestick piece of *Gothick* Architecture, compar'd with a neat Modern building : The latter is more elegant and glaring, but the former is more strong and more solemn. It must be allow'd that in one of these there are materials enough to make many of the other. It has much the greater variety, and much the nobler apartments ; tho' we are often conducted to them by dark, odd and uncouth passages. Nor does the Whole fail to strike us with greater reverence, tho' many of the Parts are childish, ill-plac'd, and unequal to its grandeur.'

Pope's poetical work is not the whole of his

life. Nor is it, as we are often inclined to think, the dominant force in the poetry of his own time. It is one among many, and his success does not establish a ruling tradition, except for the mechanic warblers. Already in the time of Dryden there were signs of novelty coming on : Atterbury (or the author of the Life of Waller, 1690) recommends blank verse—and Thomson takes the advice. Young competes with Pope in Satire and leaves this for an original policy of his own in the *Night Thoughts*. Prior commanded lyrical forms of Satire unfamiliar to Pope.

> Now let us look for Louis' feather,
> That used to shine so like a star :
> The generals could not get together,
> Wanting that influence great in war.
> O Poet ! thou hadst been discreeter,
> Hanging the Monarch's hat so high,
> If thou had'st dubb'd thy star a meteor,
> That did but blaze, and rove, and die !

Gay's address to Pope on the completion of the *Iliad*—'Mr. Pope's welcome from Greece'—is a fresh invention, in the light octaves of Italian burlesque poetry, such as had never been tried in English before, such as the English of Gay's time left unrepeated, to be taken up long after by Frere and Byron :

Cheer up, my friend, thy dangers now are o'er;
  Methinks—nay sure, the rising coasts appear ;
Hark, how the guns salute from either shore,
  As thy trim vessel cuts the Thames so fair :
Shouts answering shouts from Kent and Essex roar,
  And bells break loud from ev'ry gust of air :
Bonfires do blaze, and bones and cleavers ring,
As at the coming of some mighty king.

It is no depreciation of Pope to recognize that
there were other fashions of poetry available in
his day. On the contrary, it was a superstitious
and exclusive admiration and following of Pope
that so long prevented and to this day prevents
a right understanding of his varieties of mood and
phrase. Dr. Johnson knew better : this is his
description of ' an intelligence perpetually on the
wing, excursive, vigourous, and diligent, eager to
pursue knowledge, and attentive to retain it.'

' Of his intellectual character, the constituent and
fundamental principle was good sense, a prompt and
intuitive perception of consonance and propriety. He
saw immediately of his own conceptions what was to
be chosen and what to be rejected, and in the works
of others what was to be shunned and what was to
be copied.

' But good sense alone is a sedate and quiescent
quality, which manages its possessions well but does
not increase them ; it collects few materials for its
own operations, and preserves safety but never gains

supremacy. Pope had likewise genius; a mind active, ambitious and adventurous, always investigating, always aspiring; in its widest searches still longing to go forward, in its highest flights still wishing to be higher; always imagining something greater than it knows, always endeavouring more than it can do.'

Dr. Johnson, who found the right words exactly for the terror and beauty of the Isle of Skye, for the religion of Iona, seems here to have read truly the mind of another Adventurer.

MOLIÈRE AND THE MUSE OF COMEDY[1]

THE name of poet is taken rather loosely sometimes, especially in other languages than English : in Germany the novelist is reckoned a *Dichter*, and in Denmark Hans Andersen is a poet in his novels and fairy tales, apart from what he wrote in verse. Chateaubriand is frequently a poet in France, though his admirers think not highly of his experiments in metre : whether he or Carlyle be the worse composer of verse is a difficult and unnecessary question. Molière has the Muse of Comedy to take care of him ; does that make him a poet ? There is a Muse of History, we know, but her true servants are generally best in 'the other harmony of prose'. Is the Comic Poet, in the old sense of the word, that is to say the author of Comedies, a poet in the true sense of Poetry ? Molière's title has been canvassed ; sometimes perhaps too zealously supported by those who would make him the chief poet of France ; sometimes too bluntly

[1] Reprinted by permission from *The French Quarterly*.

denied altogether. His friend Boileau in his
second *Satire* (à M. Molière, 1664) seems to have
no doubt :

> Rare et fameux Esprit, dont la fertile veine
> Ignore en écrivant le travail et la peine,
> Pour qui tient Apollon tous ses trésors ouverts,
> Et qui sçais à quel coin se marquent les bons vers,
> Dans les combats d'esprit sçavant Maistre d'escrime,
> Enseigne-moi, Molière, où tu trouves la rime.

He praises Molière incidentally for his wit and
skill in comic debate, but it is Molière's poetry
that he chooses for his theme, for his admiration.
None of the treasures of Apollo are refused to
Molière ; he is an artist in verse and a genius in
rhyme. No doubt this praise of rhyme has its
satirical motive, and Boileau's depreciation of his
own talent in comparison with Molière's, his
complaint that it is grief and sorrow to him to
work with rhyme, is intended to lead up to the
gibe which is the real point of the satire :

> Si je veux d'un galant dépeindre la figure,
> Ma plume pour rimer trouve l'Abbé de Pure ;
> Si je pense exprimer un Auteur sans défaut,
> La raison dit Virgile et la rime Quinaut.

This no doubt is what led the author of *Hudi-
bras* to translate this *Satire*. It was not published
in his lifetime ; only in his *Remains*. It is one of
the early communications of Molière to England,

and the earliest English translation of Boileau.
It is a pity it was not better known in the reign
of Charles II. It is not obviously and openly an
English salute to Molière ; Molière's name is
suppressed, and Butler's translation is written up
to the English example which he puts in place
of Boileau's Quinaut :

> When I would praise an author, the untoward
> Damn'd sense says Virgil, but the rhyme —

The rhyme says ' Howard ', you are to understand : a blank is left, but it is easy to fill up for
any one who knows the reputation in those days
of Edward Howard and his *British Princes*.
Molière is not mentioned : but after all, we have
not the translation as Butler would have passed
it for press. He does not transpose it all to
English ground ; he repeats Boileau's original
contempt for Scudéry and translates :

> O happy Scudéry ! whose easy quill
> Can once a month a mighty volume fill ;

and it is possible that if he had printed it he
would have given the name of Molière to explain
the address with which it opens :

> Great famous Wit, whose rich and easy vein
> Free and unus'd to drudgery and pain
> Has all Apollo's treasure at command.

The English poet at any rate himself knew that

Boileau was writing to Molière, and thus we in England have some part in the contemporary praise of Molière the poet, the master of verse ; as we have on the other hand rather too much in our account set down on the other side—the depreciation of French verse and particularly of French rhyming plays. Matthew Arnold is the most exacting of critics here, and the least easily pleased. His essay on the French play in London, 1879, has a curious way of praising Molière, by arguing that French verse is essentially an erroneous form in an unsuitable language ; an impediment in Molière's freedom of speech. Molière's style is not at its best in the *Misanthrope* or *Tartuffe* ; these are rhyming plays, and no French author can make much of rhyme. Look for Molière's strength in his prose : in *L'Avare*, in the *Fourberies de Scapin*, in *Georges Dandin*. And the critic takes occasion to assert that all French verse is inept, more particularly in Victor Hugo ; which he has no difficulty in proving by his favourite device of quotation ; such as he employed to dishonour the traditional ballads and to challenge the poetry of Pope. As he took for a specimen of Pope the couplet about Hounslow Heath and Banstead Down :

Thence comes your mutton, and these chicks my own,

as for ballad poetry he ignored *Chevy Chase*, *Sir*

Patrick Spens, and *Jamie Telfer of the Dodheid,*
quoting as an example of ballad style :

When the tinker did dine he had plenty of wine,

so here to test the French Alexandrine he does
not call up the trumpets of the *Cid,*

Paraissez, Navarrais, Maures et Castillans !

nor the flute notes

Cette obscure clarté qui tombe des étoiles,

but the most commonplace couplets he can find.
The *saeva indignatio* of Alceste does not ring in
his ears :

Je ne trouve partout que lâche flatterie,
Qu'injustice, intérêt, trahison, fourberie ;
Je n'y puis plus tenir, j'enrage, et mon dessein
Est de rompre en visière à tout le genre humain.

His attitude to French verse is like that of
M. Cardinal to Rome : ' You will see ', he said
to his admiring wife, ' Rome will leave me cold.'
' Just so,' says Madame, reporting the conversation : ' Rome left him cold.'

We need not pause to meet his arguments and
explode his quotations ; let us take for granted
that Corneille and Racine were poets. Let me
be allowed a digression here, in the style of
Hazlitt, in honour of Racine, to show that
pleasant things will happen to lovers of poetry,

if they live long enough. It was on the 30th of April in the year 1921 as I was walking over a hill in Berkshire, in the land of the *Scholar Gipsy*, that I came on a notice advertising a performance of Racine's *Esther* in English. This of course was Mr. John Masefield taking his own where he found it : he has found it, on occasion, in the *Laxdæla Saga* ; he finds it now in Racine.

Let us not quarrel with Boileau's appreciation of Molière. Molière for him is a poet, showing his talent and his art in the ease and fluency of his language, in the rhymes that spring of themselves, in answer to his thought. The contrast is given with the bad poet who has a ready-made stock of commonplace rhymes and phrases. The bad poet is identified as Ménage by the commentators, Ménage who some years later turns into Vadius of the *Femmes savantes*. It is pleasant to find Boileau, the disciplinarian, praising the true life of poetry in the quick readiness, grace and ease of Molière's rhyming dialogue : we recognize the same sort of life in Chaucer, and we call it poetry, though it has not the splendours of Carlyle or Chateaubriand.

Molière's use of prose is a subject for the historians of French drama : English readers take from them the fact that prose was not commonly preferred by the audiences, and that after Molière's time the *Festin de Pierre* kept the stage in the rhyming version, not in the prose of Molière's *Don Juan.* Prose was authorized, more or less, for scholars by the Italian classical comedies, and for the vulgar by the farces : Molière used prose for the early comic pieces of his travelling company : later, he was sometimes driven to prose by want of time ; in the *Princesse d'Élide* he puts a note at the beginning of the second Act to explain that he had intended to write it all in verse but was not allowed time enough ; the rest is in prose. Few English readers will be much concerned with the motives of Molière's change from the one form to the other ; prose or verse, it is generally good enough for them : no more do they trouble themselves over the prose of Benedick and Beatrice ; the author made it so and there is little wrong with it. Nor will many agree with Matthew Arnold that Molière comes out better in *L'Avare* and *Georges Dandin* than in *Tartuffe* and the *Misanthrope.* But we may say that Molière did not write in prose only when the King left too short a time for rehearsals. *Les Précieuses ridicules* could not have been anything other than it is. It would no more do in verse than the speeches of Mrs. Jennings or Mrs. Norris, the letters of Mr. Collins. We all believe the story of the old man who called out from the parterre at the end of this short play : ' Courage, Molière, voilà la bonne comédie ! ' and so say we all very heartily. It is a new thing, ordinary speech raised to the highest degree of comic meaning. In two other later pieces of prose dialogue Molière may be found even better : in *La Critique de l'École des Femmes* and in *L'Impromptu de Versailles*, the *Critique* showing all the best people engaged in discussing Molière's questionable manners and vulgar ideas, the *Impromptu* bringing forward Molière in his own person as manager driven nearly out of his wits by the business of managing. Here indeed in prose there is something that no verse can give, no more than verse would do for Hamlet's conversation with the Players, which is the nearest thing in English to those reflections of Molière on the problems of the stage. No ! we cannot allow *L'Avare* and *Georges Dandin* to be put against the two great rhyming comedies ; but we find in the *Critique* and the *Impromptu* the true mind of the author behind the scenes, not better nor worse than in the great plays, but differently expressed ; no more to be compared with his greater works than Keats's letters with his poetry, but telling, like Keats's letters, what the poems do not think of expressing. At the same time the *Critique* and the *Impromptu* with

all their personal remarks belong to the world of
comedy ; the *Critique* especially is a rendering
of good society as complete in its way as the
Misanthrope, comprehending more than *Les
Femmes savantes*. Part of Molière's influence
and authority is won through his confidences ;
we applaud his plays, but not impartially, as if
the author were unknown to us. He compels us
to follow and understand the troubles of his pro-
fessional life, the aim and scope of his art. This
is not done through reminiscences, like those of
Hazlitt or Stevenson, nor in prefaces like those
of Corneille, Dryden, or Henry James, but through
drama : the text and the commentary are all one,
and nowhere, unless it be in the *Impromptu*, is
his dialogue more lively and spirited than in his
comedy on comedy, the *Critique de l'École des
Femmes*. One of the ladies in that play I wish
to name particularly with great respect : Élise,
who is all good sense and humour ; Élise deals
with Climène, the languishing affected conventional lady, as Swift's Stella was accustomed in
conversation to deal with fools ; agreeing with
them and letting them have their own way.

The *Critique de l'École des Femmes* if it is not
a regular comedy may claim consideration on
other grounds. It does not matter much what
you call it, we are not concerned to name and

label species and varieties ; but the likeness of
Molière to Plato in this dialogue ought not to
be forgotten : the study of dramatic form, the
history of the theatre, may sometimes lead to
neglect of the pure comedy in Plato's dialogues.
As the comic motive in those is usually the
display of intellectual, and sometimes of learned
and literary vanities, and always the refutation of
various limited minds, so here Dorante, who
represents Molière, has to argue against the pre-
judices of taste in polite society ; in so doing he
brings out his own theory and principles. Incidentally the likeness is often very close in detail ;
Plato's parody of artistic prose in *Gorgias* and the
Symposium is the same kind of thing as Molière's
criticism of literary conceits, as Shakespeare's
continual ridicule of pretentious language, from
Don Adriano to Osric and later. But Dorante
and Molière in this piece have another object ;
nothing less than a complete theory of comic
drama, the relation of drama to the audience and
to real life. He turns away from the conceits of
the *Précieuses* to say what he thinks about his
own life as a writer of comedies. It is impossible
to make an abstract of this quintessence ; it
explains itself, and there is nothing superfluous in
it. Two things in argument are notable perhaps
more than the rest. Molière, the King's servant,

who had been advised by Boileau to keep his
attention on the life of the Court, and who
actually in this present comedy is representing
the world of good manners and fine shades—
Molière refuses to leave the final judgement of
a play to the boxes ; good sense, good taste, he
says, are the same, whatever they may pay at the
door ; a marquis is not entitled to dictate to
the man in the pit. Molière remembered his
unknown friend in the parterre at the *Précieuses
ridicules*.

This is good enough, and it would not have
been said if Molière had not believed it. His
work, with all its dependence on the King and
the Court, is not court poetry ; he writes for
every one. The other point is of far greater
importance. We are not surprised or offended
to hear that the pit may often be right, whatever
Hamlet may say in contempt of the groundlings,
or Ben Jonson of the many-headed bench. But
to this day it has not been fully recognized what
meaning there is in Dorante's assertion and claim
that comedy is more difficult than tragedy. It
is a flash of lightning ; Molière has invented
' a new thrill ' : his sentence is as strange, as full
of meaning, as that last word of Socrates at the
end of supper, after the play, talking to Agathon
the tragic poet and Aristophanes : that the poet

of tragedy ought to be the poet of comedy too :
a prophecy not fulfilled in his day nor in Plato's.
Molière's opinion is even more amazing. Tragedy
is easier than comedy. It must therefore be
easier to find, there must be more good tragedies
in the world than comedies. Many of us have
thought so, even without Meredith's essay on
Comedy to influence us ; after that argument
one is ready to copy Rasselas and say : ' Enough :
thou hast persuaded us that no one ever wrote
a thoroughly true comedy, sound and right in all
respects : except Molière in the *Misanthrope*, and
probably Congreve in the *Way of the World*.'
This perhaps is going a little too far, but that
is the direction. If one accepts Meredith's conditions and postulates, it is not easy to find many
thoroughly good comedies. For comedy, he
requires society not only well mannered and
intelligent ; it must be perfectly balanced : the
debate of Alceste and Célimène, of Mirabel and
Millamant is impossible in Attic comedy, old or
new ; it is impossible in Rome, though thinking
of Catullus and Propertius we may conjecture
that it was the Greek conventions and not wholly
the Roman world that prevented such a theme.
Meredith's idea does not allow room for Charles
Lamb's ideal universe of artificial Comedy :
Thalia the Comic Muse has her own law which

is not that of tragedy ; which is not that of real
life either, because comedy is art, not life. But
for Meredith and for Molière the law of comedy
is closer to real life than Charles Lamb's view in
his apology. In the action of the *Misanthrope* it
is not enough for the characters to be life-like:
the whole enveloping atmosphere is life-like, and
as much a part of the play as the tragic destinies
of Thebes or Verona, as the burden of mystery
in *Macbeth*.

Are we expected to think that Molière in the
Misanthrope has killed all his rivals in comedy ?
no brothers near his throne ? He himself would
have been sorry to think so, with *Tartuffe* and
Don Juan, *L'Avare* and *Scapin* and the *Femmes
savantes*, and so much more to come. Molière's
own world had been discovered by Shakespeare,
the perfect balance of good society in *Love's
Labour's Lost*. Where in those Elizabethan days
did he discover the finer shades ? In Spain there
were scores, hundreds, of good comedies beside
those which gave Corneille more than the plot
of *Le Menteur*, to Thomas Corneille his Mock
Astrologer, his *Amour à la Mode*, to Molière his
Don Juan. After Molière we can all think of
two or three comedies not far short of the best.
For a keyword of Comedy there is nothing in
Molière more significant than in the *Barbier de*

Séville—' Qui diable est-ce qu'on trompe ici ? '—
and the *Mariage de Figaro* is not far from the
Absolute. Yet the *Misanthrope* stands out, for
those who have once been made free of that
drawing-room, as something different from all the
rest. It may be enthusiasm, fanaticism—it may
be unjust to Molière himself to think so—but
Alceste and Célimène are personages whom one
takes in a different way from any other. They
are not characters of tragedy, nor do they belong
to actual history; they are subjects of Thalia
and all that we know of them is their rhythmical
movement in the dance that their poet and leader
has so craftily invented and conducted. Yet we
find ourselves wondering about them as if they
were actual problems of history or of contemporary life. Molière has led his Mistress, the
Comic Muse, to the very end of her world;
another step and there is either full reality or
mere blank nonentity—either Alceste and Célimène with a great deal more to say for themselves than their actual words in the play, or else
only the reproving voice of the Master of the
Show, telling the innocent spectators that they
have had enough for their money, and that they
had better go home and read the fable of Rosa-
mond and the Purple Jar. Still, we are not
content; and whatever the meaning, value, and

purport of this remarkable comedy may be, it is
a thing that keeps the spectator inevitably wanting
to know more than he is told about the two
adversaries. Saint-Évremond—I meant to speak
of him later, but he is relevant here—Saint-
Évremond in his comparison of French and
English drama, which is really a comparison of
France and England, says that while the French
often do not think enough, the English on the
contrary sometimes think too deep ; they go on
digging, he says, when there is nothing more to
be found. That may be what I have been doing
now, and it may be futile to look for more in
a play than the author chooses to give. But then
Molière in the *Misanthrope* does give us exactly
this problem. My own opinion is that Célimène
has been treated unfairly. Her critical remarks
on her friends are not supposed to be untrue
calumnies ; Élise, the amiable lady of whom I have
already spoken, in the *Critique,* is not sincere, and
her ironical flattery would not be spared by
Alceste any more than the character sketches of
Célimène. Célimène is not refuted utterly by
Alceste : she might have a very good answer
ready for his last appeal. Molière and the Comic
Genius know where Alceste is wrong ; the freedom of Célimène even in her malice might be
an antidote to the self-centred self-will of her

opposite, whose generous mind will hardly consider it possible that he may be mistaken. Do
any of us think more highly of this lady than her
author intends ? It does not really matter ; the
meaning of works of art is not limited by what their
authors intend: the towers of Oxford have innumerable lights and shades that were not in the mind
of their architects, and poems may gain in beauty
through successive generations of readers. And I
will maintain that Molière's great comedy is not
best understood by judging this lady to be no more
than an example of treachery. Without any far-
fetched refinement of criticism at all we can
quote the speeches where Célimène is all on the
side of good sense against Arsinoé the prude ;
Molière is not the man to forget or to dishonour
any character who has come out as a debater on
his own side.

After the *Misanthrope* the other plays seem less
interesting ; the more regular comedies, *L'Avare*
and *Les Femmes savantes*, too simple in their
problems ; the farces of *Scapin* and the *Malade
imaginaire*, good enough to laugh at on the stage,
but living in the memory through their actors,
if they are remembered at all. It is impossible
to compare them with the wit, humour, and grace
of the *Critique* and the *Impromptu*, and for pure
laughter the irregular scenes of *Les Fâcheux*, the

various bores, are incalculably richer and more profitable, the hunting man and the man who insists in telling over his unlucky hand at piquet.

Mr. Arthur Tilley in his excellent book, lately published, on Molière uses in one place the term Aristophanic of his author, but goes no further. It is the right word for *Les Fâcheux* and for other things in Molière : there is nothing in Molière's bores (the word, by the way, is Sir Walter Scott's in his Life of Molière, speaking a good deal to the point of *Les Fâcheux*), there is nothing here specially of the new Comedy, nothing of the dramatic rules and unities. Aristophanes could and did bring on and off ridiculous personages when he chose with no more plan or plot than Molière in this nightmare succession of bores. Do we see now something to explain why good regular comedies are so hard to find ? Is not the reason simply that comedy can thrive without a plot, in scenes, sketches, speeches ? Is this blasphemy against the Comic Muse, a denial of the claims of art ?

I propose a theory which, whether scientific or not, has the merit of 'saving the appearances', in the old scholastic sense, that is, of not leaving anything disregarded.

My theory is this : that besides Thalia the Muse there is the god Dionysus still alive and perpetually interested in Comedy. He will go any length for Tragedy also, as we know from the *Frogs* ; but we know from the *Frogs* that he expects the poets to work for him in Tragedy ; with Comedy he does not leave everything to the Muse. He is always capable of interfering. He is not really the Dionysus of the *Frogs* ; to see what he is you must go to the *Bacchae* of Euripides. He is a jealous young unscrupulous god, and in Comedy he has no respect for the Unities. He made Falstaff and turned him loose in an historical tragedy. The Muse Thalia rescued him for her regular comedy *The Merry Wives* ; the god was delighted to see what she made of it. His Comedy is the old Comedy, his poet is Aristophanes. He may be traced occasionally in French comedy before Molière. Surely Desmarests de Saint-Sorlin is Aristophanes in his *Visionnaires*, particularly in the opening scene : enter Miles Gloriosus with a long tirade of his valour and achievements, such as we have heard before ; but then, to him enter a Poet declaiming in the style of Du Bartas, plenty of compound epithets after the old fashion, and the Hero grows pale at this prodigy and runs away. This is the work of Dionysus. He is very evident in the *Menteur* of Corneille, as he was in the original Spanish of Alarcón, *La Verdad sospechosa*. The

plot is poor, rather, in Spanish and in French ;
but when the Liar is at his best, and that was
when Delaunay acted him forty years ago and
more, we could not doubt the god was there.
He stood at the front of the stage, inventing ;
you almost saw the amazing fiction springing up
and round him like the miracle of the vine played
on the Tuscan mariners. All the time at the
back of the scene the ingenious servant was
crouching, all his usual conventional craft dis-
comfited in this irruption of a more glorious
power. Then the dramatist left to himself makes
a wrong ending. The Liar is confounded ; nevertheless he and Dionysus have had their hour, and
that is what we remember, that lives, and the
plot of the play is forgotten.

So in Molière we need not be much distressed
if the Miser, a comedy, is defeated by the Bores,
a string of monologues, or by the *Impromptu*,
which is Molière the actor-manager and his company, acting themselves. We cannot see or hear
it all at this distance, but the *Impromptu* is still
not only the liveliest of Molière's pieces, but
a thing unequalled anywhere. We cannot see
and hear Molière doing imitations of favourite
actors, but we see and hear him, distracted, calling
his people together, as usual with no time and
as usual with the actors all going different ways,

'a pretty lot of animals to drive' says the actor-
manager : and this was said in the presence of
the King as well as of all the company who acted
this rehearsal before him. Do the King and the
Court escape ? Molière explains to his people
how high and difficult his task is, producing
comedies for the great people 'who will not
laugh unless they want to'. The play itself,
where Molière acts one foolish Marquis arguing
with another which of them was the original of
the foolish Marquis in the *Critique*, need not now
be discussed : it is enough, for the present, to
see that Molière is playing very cleverly several
games at once—defence of himself, satirical
comedy, and, best of all, his own mind, character,
and anxieties. That last is his strongest spell ;
it may be an unfair one, but then Dionysus is
unfair. This poet is liked all over the world
because we have seen him in a bad temper with
his animals of comedians, and doing his best for
them all the time.

I end with a mention of two praises of Molière
written in this country : Andrew Lang's letter
to M. de Molière, Valet de Chambre du Roy,
and Saint-Évremond's notice of him, very short
and complete. Saint-Évremond, I may say, has
some share in him of the old Comedy : his
Académiciens is said to have suggested to Molière

the quarrel of Trissotin and Vadius, and later his *Sir Politick Would-Be, comédie à la manière des Anglais,* written along with the Duke of Buckingham, has at least one character of merit : the German traveller in Venice with his note-book, who does not like to waste his time : ' Conversation ! what have I to do with conversation ? I want to see the Monuments ! ' He had been in Oxford and remembered Guy Fawkes's lantern there, among the monuments. This is his first appearance on any stage, and he is recognizable.

Saint-Évremond's opinion is given thus in the title of an essay :

Sur nos comédies, exceptées celles de Molière, où l'on trouve le vrai Esprit de la Comédie.

It is not a showy epigram, but it is just what he thought, and it is true enough.

MATTHEW ARNOLD

I CANNOT begin this lecture without a word in memory of Walter Raleigh, but let me say at once that I have no funeral sermon to pronounce, and that even if I had at command the noblest of prose sentences about life and death I would not speak them. For it seems to me, thinking much about him since I saw him last on the 7th of May, that Walter Raleigh understood those matters—laments, elegies, funeral orations—better than any one I have known. He knew that the best interpretation comes through poetry; and that 'consolatories writ with studied argument' in prose are a pretence and makeshift between two realities: the immediate shock of grief which has no words to express it, and the other real world of *Lycidas*, *Thyrsis*, or the epilogue to *Sohrab and Rustum*. Raleigh wrote to me once: 'We never get used to death; if we did it would mean that we were not ourselves alive.' With that in mind, and considering also how quick he was to detect false rhetoric and the wrong kinds of solemnity, I will say only that he would be glad to be remembered here as we remember him. He was pleased when he found that I had quoted some rhymes of his in my *Dark Ages*: I have read them again lately, and I will repeat them.

They were written in imitation of a quaint old
Irish stanza :

> Though our songs
> Cannot banish ancient wrongs,
> Though they follow where the rose
>   goes :
> And their sound,
> Swooning over hollow ground,
> Fades, and leaves the enchanted air
>   bare :
> Yet the wise
> Say that not unblest he dies
> Who has known a single May
>   day :
> If we have laughed,
> Loved, and laboured in our craft,
> We may pass with a resigned
>   mind.

He has put all his world into this, and it is very
like him.

MATTHEW ARNOLD came out as a poet in the
Sheldonian Theatre on the 28th of June 1843,
having won Sir Roger Newdigate's prize. *Cromwell* was the subject : the motto is from Schiller :

> Schrecklich ist es deiner Wahrheit
> Sterbliches Gefäss zu seyn.

The poem begins with an allusion to the idea
expressed in the twelfth of Mr. Wordsworth's
sonnets to Liberty :

> Two voices are there; one is of the sea,

contrasting it with the fact of Cromwell's birth-place having been the fen country of Huntingdon-shire, where he lived till he was forty years old.

The opening is rather remote from Oliver Cromwell, but it is a fair prophecy of Arnold's later poetry—his vision of life between the mountains and the sea, and of life which is deeper than the sea. He has been one of our own poets ever since. He lived (he is reported to have said), he and Clough and another friend, in Oxford as if it were a great country house: his praise of Oxford is well remembered, and keeps alive an Oxford still recognizable, in spite of the thin ends of wedges and the thick of unnecessary suburbs. He claims, and has, our loyalty through the religion of the place, which none of us will blame as superstitious. If we are partisans of our poet, we hope we can justify our regard in the eye of the pure Reason. We must of course be careful not to fall into the common snare of impartiality in this country, which has been described in the sentence: ' An Englishman never thinks he is really impartial till he has voted against his better judgement.'

A good deal of plain unprejudiced truth has been spoken about Matthew Arnold by some of his best friends and most sincere admirers. If I should take up any of the business of the Devil's

Advocate, it will not be for more than a short spell of debate on points where the challenge comes first from himself, and, in any case, with a full sense of the danger of such controversy.

Let me make some amends, if I may, for some things that I have said, not quite exactly true, in referring to some of Arnold's critical opinions. The preface to *Merope* shows the same prejudice against French dramatic verse as the essay twenty years later on the French Play in London; but in that preface he declares his belief in the poetical beauty of Racine more definitely than I had remembered. And when I said, speaking of his unfair quotations, that he ignored the true beauty of the ballads, as for example *Sir Patrick Spens*, when he quoted as specimens of ballad style :

> Now Christ thee save thou proud porter,
> Now Christ thee save and see !

and the other too notorious verse about the tinker, I forgot a later passage in the lectures on translating Homer : ' By the occurrence of this lyrical cry the ballad poets themselves rise sometimes, though not so often as one might perhaps have hoped, to the grand style.' Then he quotes :

> O lang, lang may the ladies sit
> Wi' their fans into their hand
> Or ere they see Sir Patrick Spence
> Come sailing to the land—

and the verse following; which takes off something from the unfairness of the tinker.

It is not my purpose to say more about Arnold's critical judgements on poetry except where they touch on his own intentions and performance, as in the preface to his Poems dated October 1853, and the preface to *Merope*, December 1857.

The preface of 1853 seems to me nearly perfect in doctrine. It gives unanswerably good reasons for the withdrawal of *Empedocles on Etna*; reasons with nothing wrong in them except that they withdraw *Empedocles*. They are none the worse, in principle, as we take them now, with *Empedocles* restored to a place in the volume of Arnold's poetry.

There are two chief points in the argument here: one, that all true poetry is exhilarating: 'it is demanded not only that it shall interest, but also that it shall inspirit and rejoice the reader: that it shall convey a charm and infuse delight'. The poetry of spiritual anxiety, indecision, mere mental distress, is not the right sort of poetry. 'What are the situations from the representation of which, though accurate, no poetical enjoyment can be derived? They are those in which the suffering finds no vent in action; in which a continuous state of mental distress is prolonged, unrelieved by incident, hope or resistance ; in which there is everything to be endured, nothing to be done. In such situations there is inevitably something morbid, in the description of them something monotonous. When they occur in actual life they are painful, not tragic ; the representation of them in poetry is painful also.'

This is too hard on *Empedocles*, but is it not good sense, and does it not go far ? The other main point in this preface is equally well argued. You are not to think that *Empedocles* is withdrawn through any scruple about the fitness of old Greek themes for a modern English reading public. ' It has not been excluded in deference to the opinion which many critics of the present day appear to entertain against subjects chosen from distant times and countries : against the choice, in short, of any subjects but modern ones.'

Then proceeding to perform the operation of incision into what is raw, he disposes his subject on the operating table. His demonstration is made on the body of the *Spectator* of 2 April 1853, from which he quotes : ' The Poet who would really fix the public attention must leave the exhausted past and draw his subjects from matters of present import, and therefore both of interest and novelty.' Seventy years ago this *blague* was frequent : ' a fair example of a class of critical *dicta* everywhere current at the present day, having a philosophical form and air, but no real basis in fact; and which are calculated to vitiate the judgment of readers of poetry, while they exert, so far as they are adopted, a misleading influence on the practice of those who write it.'

Matthew Arnold's quotation from the *Spectator* is convenient for reference, and may be used to complete the great encyclopaedia of Cant which Flaubert began. It may be supported by a late distinguished American author who went ecstatic over Mark Twain's *Yankee at the Court of King Arthur*, as bringing out the greater, truer heart of our time—so much better worth thinking about than Percival or Galahad. It ought to be observed that Arnold's protest is very far from meaning exclusive preference of ancient noble legendary themes for poetry: it does not touch Wordsworth's *Michael*.

How good and sane is Arnold's description of the poets who have learned their art from the ancients! 'They do not talk of their mission, nor of interpreting their age, nor of the coming Poet; all this, they know, is the mere delirium of vanity; their business is not to praise their age, but to afford to the men who live in it the highest pleasure which they are capable of feeling.' The strange thing about this very admirable preface is that while it explains so well the meaning and value of the ancient stories, nothing is said about *Sohrab and Rustum, Tristram and Yseult, The Neckan, The Forsaken Merman*, poems that follow and make a large part of the book. The author probably thought that sensible readers could be trusted to make out for themselves what his policy was. A note to *Sohrab and Rustum* (1854) shows that not all his critics were sensible or even honest : to defeat their misunderstanding and misrepresentation he gives an account of his sources ; but he does not think fit to say a word about his poetical aim or his employment of the classical epic forms on a subject from Firdausi. This simply as a matter of biography and of Arnold's opinions is curious, for the preface to *Merope* shows that he was still more or less a believer in the simple theory of a classical and a romantic school :

> ' Whatever the critics may say, there exists, I am convinced, in England, even in this stronghold of the romantic school, a wide though an ill-informed curiosity on the subject of the so-called classical school, meriting a more complete satisfaction than it has hitherto obtained.'

Strangely naïve, for a reader of Goethe, this theory of the two schools—a theory refuted

implicitly in *Sohrab and Rustum*. That anything
may be classical if it is treated in the right way
is Goethe's decision on the problem. This is
what Landor's argument comes to, in his letter
to the Author of *Festus* which was printed in
Last Fruit off an old Tree, 1853 :

> We talk of schools . . . unscholarly, if schools
> Part the romantic from the classical.
> The classical, like the heroick age,
> Is past ; but Poetry may reassume
> That glorious name with Tartar and with Turk,
> With Goth or Arab, Sheik or Paladin,
> And not with Roman and with Greek alone.
> The name is graven on the workmanship.
> The trumpet blast of *Marmion* never shook
> The God-built walls of Ilion ; yet what shout
> Of the Achaians swells the heart so high?
> Nor fainter is the artillery roar that booms
> From *Hohenlinden* to the *Baltick* strand.
> Shakespeare with majesty benign call'd up
> The obedient classicks from their marble seat
> And led them through dim glen and sheeny glade
> And over precipices, over seas
> Unknown by mariner, to palaces
> High archt, to festival, to dance, to joust,
> And steeds that Pheidias had turn'd pale to see.

' The name is graven on the workmanship ' : the
Persian story of Sohrab and Rustum is as classical
in Arnold's poem as his tragedy of *Merope*.

Some readers find the poem too artificial : epic poetry according to receipt. The word *pastiche* has been used to express what some of the cavillers mean. It is worth considering, for there is a good deal to be said on behalf of the cavillers. I think they are wrong, but wrong only if they depreciate the poem and renounce its beauty because of its Homeric or Virgilian echoes : not wrong in saying that the poem is artifice. Of course it is artifice ; and so are some of the finest things in modern poetry. *The Ancient Mariner* is openly a got-up thing, even a parody. If Coleridge took away the quaint spelling of the first edition (*Ancyent Marinere*, 1798) and put ' ghastly ' in place of ' eldritch ' and ' given ' for ' yeven '—

To Mary Queen the praise be yeven (1798)

—he added later the prose marginal gloss, which serves more purposes than one, but one of them certainly is to give more of an old-fashioned air to the poem through the parody of old English prose that accompanies it. (A malediction here on the pedantry that has made it impossible to speak of an old English ballad, and hardly of an old English gentleman, without explaining that you do not mean Anglo-Saxon !)

The Lays of Ancient Rome are also parody : and

it is through neglect of this that Arnold is so
unjust to *Horatius* :

> Then out spake brave Horatius,
>   The captain of the gate :
> ' To every man upon this earth
>   Death cometh soon or late '—

Arnold seems to take this as a poetical paraphrase
of the well-known fact that all men are mortal.
But is it not right enough if you accept the
convention of ballad poetry, even as in the
Ancyent Marinere ?   By itself the meaning is
flat : but it is not here by itself, and to take it
apart from the conclusion, and to forget that it
is drama, is wrong criticism.

> ' And how can man die better
>   Than facing fearful odds,
> For the ashes of his fathers
>   And the temples of his gods? '

Is it impertinent to say here—I find it myself
rather pleasant—that three of the greatest admirers of Matthew Arnold's poetry are also the
strongest advocates of the *Lays of Ancient Rome* ?
The Professor of Latin at Cambridge will forgive
me if I mention that the author of *A Shropshire
Lad* is one of them.

I cannot explain what I think about *Sohrab and
Rustum* till I have said something about *Merope*.

The tragedy of *Merope*, with its preface, seems to
me to be one of those strange ' visitings ' that
have to be noted along with the inspiration of
the Muses : besides the Muses there are Powers
of the air, *aeria animalia,* ' eyrisshe bestes ', as
Chaucer calls them ; demons, in short, that
occasionally fill the minds even of good artists
with vanity. *Merope* is a return to the worst
idolatry of the Renaissance, the belief in the
formal pattern, especially of classical drama. It
is touching to see the poet struggling with the
enemy. The light that leads astray is light from
Heaven ; the poet sets out from true sincere
worship of Greek tragedy, and his enterprise is no
mean one : to express the beauty of Greek form
in English verse. But then he falls into the cold
empty space, where nothing lives but vacuity,
the pithless phantoms of mere Form. He has
no subject in his mind, and he comforts himself by
observing that

> ' It remained to select a subject from among those
> which had been considered to possess the true requisites
> of good tragic subjects ; on which great works had
> been composed, but had not survived to chill emula-
> tion by their grandeur. Of such subjects there is
> fortunately no lack. In the writings of Hyginus, a
> Latin mythographer of uncertain date, we possess
> a large stock of them.'

It is very strange. The tragic poet who is going to reproduce for modern England the glory of Greek tragedy does not know what his story is going to be ; he is in possession of a classical blank diagram, and is comforted when he thinks of the large stock of subjects in Hyginus. If Matthew Arnold in another frame of mind had come upon this sentence in another poet's preface, would he not have made play with this Latin mythographer of uncertain date, and his large stock of subjects warranted good for tragedy ? We know exactly how the phrase would fall, repeated each time with increasing enjoyment.

The 'large stock' of Hyginus makes one think of Milton's list of tragic subjects, and his choice long wavering over one or another of them. But Milton's tragedy when it came at last was only done because the story took hold of Milton's mind : *Samson Agonistes* was not chosen from the large stock to exemplify the form of Greek drama.

Discussion of poetic form is apt to be tedious, but that cannot be helped. If Poetry be a fit subject for Academic lectures, surely form must always be the main part of the business. There is nothing more important for the understanding of poetry than a study of form, and no better summary of it all than the phrase of Horace (Corneille's motto for his *Cinna*) :

— cui lecta potenter erit res,
nec facundia deseret hunc nec lucidus ordo.

The poet who puts all his heart into his plot will find his work done for him : the story provides him with the right words and the right proportions.

The fault of the drama of *Merope* is that the fable is not *lecta potenter*. It is merely found suitable ; the author does not take it to heart, and it does not carry the author with it.

Corneille's motto is true of Racine. Racine does not keep a list, a large stock of subjects. Racine, the only modern poet who has made all his living out of Greek tragedy, takes the stories of Euripides—*Andromache, Iphigenia, Hippolytus* —and lets them fill his imagination ; then they find their form. If in these, and in his other plays not Greek in subject, he uses what may be called a formula of dramatic construction, so does Shakespeare, whose mode of work is essentially the same as Racine's, only he has a greater variety of formulas, and changes his design with every subject. Is this not the way of all great poets and all fine poems ? It is the way of Matthew Arnold in *Empedocles, Sohrab and Rustum, The Forsaken Merman, The Scholar Gipsy,* and *Thyrsis.*

The poet who believes so strongly, so rightly and truly, in the force of Greek tradition, the irresistible value of Greek legend, takes for his epic a Persian story, *Sohrab and Rustum* ; a piece of old Northern mythology, the death of Balder. He loses much in the choice : he loses what was not lost by the authors of *Hyperion* and *Prometheus Unbound*. The scene and the story of *Sohrab and Rustum* need explaining : the story of Balder may indeed be nearer to us, nearer by ancestry, in one sense, than anything of Thebes or Troy ; but the mythology of Asgard is not really part of our inheritance, though we have rights in it. Again I say it is strange that the poet who lectured at one time on Homer, at another on the *Mabinogion*, should not have said anything, apart from citation of authorities, about his Persian and Norwegian epic poetry. Are they, as some think, artificial poetry, Homeric or Virgilian parodies ? I left this difficulty in order to speak of *Merope*, which is imitation in a different way, copying the mere abstract form ; whereas *Sohrab and Rustum* and *Balder Dead* repeat forms of imagination which have an eternally fresh life in them. *Merope*, copying Greek tragedy, uses *stichomythia*, the dialogue in single lines which is a mark of all modern classical tragedies, a fashion that has no value in it except as recalling one of the least attractive formalisms of Greek drama. *Sohrab and Rustum* is full of the epic simile— a formalism, if you will, but how different in result ! The epic simile, which Chaucer discovered in Dante and Boccaccio—for it was the new Italian poets, and not Virgil or Ovid, that proved to him its fitness for English poetry—the epic simile is one of the poetical ideas that may be new every morning, new life in the English poet's mind :

> — as at dawn
> The shepherd from his mountain lodge descries
> A far bright city, smitten by the sun,
> Through many rolling clouds, so Rustum saw
> His youth :

> — as a cunning workman in Pekin
> Pricks with vermilion some clear porcelain vase
> An emperor's gift—at early morn he paints
> And all day long, and when night comes the lamp
> Lights up his studious forehead and thin hands—
> So delicately prick'd the sign appear'd
> On Sohrab's arm, the sign of Rustum's seal.

> — Nor yet could Hermod see his brother's face
> For it grew dark ; but Hoder touch'd his arm.
> And as a spray of honeysuckle flowers
> Brushes across a tired traveller's face
> Who shuffles through the deep dew-moisten'd dust
> On a May evening, in the darken'd lanes,
> And starts him, that he thinks a ghost went by.

The formal device comes down from Homer ;

nothing in one sense has been more hackneyed in
the hands of poor poets, and few literary inventions have been so often burlesqued : yet the
Homeric simile lives on. The contrast between
this and the tragic *stichomythia* is edifying.

Sohrab and Rustum required from its author
more than a fair amount of courage. It was
nearly a desperate venture : to take a story that
no one in England could be expected to care
about, with no traditional authority round it ;
to tell it in a style that provoked at every line
the charge of Virgilian parody. The story taken
in abstract is not unlike the story of Merope.
Rustum kills his son, not knowing him. The thrill
that made the success of *Merope* in the original
Greek was Merope very nearly killing her son by
mistake. What is the difference ? The difference
is this, that what I am going to read, well known
to all of us, but never too well known to be remembered, is Matthew Arnold's *Sohrab and Rustum,*
and that there is nothing like it in his *Merope.*

> So on the bloody sand Sohrab lay dead.
> And the great Rustum drew his horseman's cloak
> Down o'er his face, and sat by his dead son.
> As those black granite pillars, once high rear'd
> By Jemshid in Persepolis, to bear
> His house, now, mid their broken flights of steps
> Lie prone, enormous, down the mountain side—
> So in the sand lay Rustum by his son.

And night came down over the solemn waste,
And the two gazing hosts, and that sole pair,
And darken'd all; and a cold fog, with night,
Crept from the Oxus. Soon a hum arose,
As of a great assembly loos'd, and fires
Began to twinkle through the fog; for now
Both armies moved to camp, and took their meal;
The Persians took it on the open sands
Southward, the Tartars by the river marge;
And Rustum and his son were left alone.

But the majestic river floated on,
Out of the mist and hum of that low land,
Into the frosty starlight, and there moved,
Rejoicing, through the hush'd Chorasmian waste,
Under the solitary moon;—he flow'd
Right for the polar star, past Orgunjè,
Brimming, and bright, and large; then sands begin
To hem his watery march, and dam his streams,
And split his currents; that for many a league
The shorn and parcell'd Oxus strains along
Through beds of sand and matted rushy isles—
Oxus, forgetting the bright speed he had
In his high mountain cradle in Pamere,
A foil'd circuitous wanderer—till at last
The long'd-for dash of waves is heard, and wide
His luminous home of waters opens, bright
And tranquil, from whose floor the new-bathed stars
Emerge, and shine upon the Aral sea.

Empedocles on Etna, we have seen, was condemned by its author for very good reasons.
Only, the reasons do not cover the whole of the

poem, and it is not really disqualified though what the author says discussing it be true and incontrovertible. ' This strange disease of modern life ' does not of itself make a tragedy. That is why Arnold condemned his poem. But there is more in *Empedocles* than the motives that led to *Obermann* and *Obermann once more*. Matthew Arnold kept the songs of Callicles when he jettisoned the drama. But the songs of Callicles lose something when they are taken by themselves ; the poems of Cadmus and Harmonia, Typho, Apollo and Marsyas, are essentially part of the lyrical drama. The drama is really a debate, and the conclusion is not the passing of Empedocles. The conclusion is what you make of it when you have read the song of Empedocles and the songs of Callicles together : the philosophic argument of the vanity of gods and men ; the poetry of the Greek legend.

The songs of Callicles are full of touches from Pindar :

> There those two live, far in the Illyrian brakes !
> They had stay'd long enough to see,
> In Thebes, the billow of calamity
> Over their own dear children roll'd,
> Curse upon curse, pang upon pang,
> For years, they sitting helpless in their home,
> A grey old man and woman ; yet of old
> The Gods had to their marriage come,
> And at the banquet all the Muses sang.

'All the Muses sang' is from the third **Pythian** ode, Arnold's favourite quotation ; it comes in the lectures on Homer, and long after in his essay on Gray :

αἰὼν δ' ἀσφαλὴς
οὐκ ἔγεντ' οὔτ' Αἰακίδᾳ παρὰ Πηλεῖ
οὔτε παρ' ἀντιθέῳ Κάδμῳ—

Chiron tutor of Achilles is from Pindar ; so also is Typho under Etna. Those beauties it may be said—the Devil's advocate is not slow to assert it—are mere literary ornaments, vanities of a late-born exhausted Alexandrian age. It may be so. Is it any valid retort to say that Homer is full of allusions to

beauty making beautiful old rhyme
In praise of ladies dead and lovely knights—

that Pindar himself knows the heroes through their poems—' Nestor and Lycian Sarpedon from the resonant verse as the craftsmen of poetry have fashioned it ' ?

The old Norse poem of the Dreams of Balder, which Gray translated in the *Descent of Odin*, is less direct in style and more allusive than *Balder Dead*. No modern poem of reminiscence, nothing of Leconte de Lisle or Heredia, is more subtle than the wonderful short dithyramb of Bacchylides, the dialogue poem of the approach of Theseus : ' Who is he that is coming from the

South, the young man who carries two javelins, flaming hair under helmet ? he is ridding the coast of foul beasts and felons, and drawing near to the bright city of Athens.' The story of Theseus was known to every mother's son in Greece : but here it is all suspense and expectation ; hardly anything left of the heroic substance, except the feeling that the Hero is abroad and is coming home. It is all new, and all wonderful ; the poem goes back for its life to the people who did not know the name of Theseus. Poetic reflection on the past, on the ' large stock ' of heroic stories, turns into this miracle of youth and hope—in four stanzas. It was not left to the Alexandrians nor to any modern Romantic or Parnassian school to discern that poetry lives on reminiscence.

There is little to tell about the *Scholar Gipsy* or *Thyrsis*. After the praise of *Thyrsis* in Swinburne's review (1867) it is not profitable to try for other words to say the same thing. There is seldom anything wrong with Swinburne's quotations from Arnold. Already in 1867 he points to Arnold's Wordsworthian phrasing :

> Yet still from time to time, vague and forlorn,
> From the soul's subterranean depth upborne
> Came airs, and floating echoes, and convey
> A melancholy into all our day.

He quotes from *Thyrsis* :

> O easy access to the hearer's grace
>   When Dorian shepherds sang to Proserpine !
>   For she herself had trod Sicilian fields,
>   She knew the Dorian water's gush divine,
>   She knew each lily white which Enna yields
>   Each rose with blushing face ;
>   She loved the Dorian pipe, the Dorian strain.
>   But ah, of our poor Thames she never heard !
>   Her foot the Cumner cowslips never stirr'd !
>   And we should tease her with our plaint in vain.

There, I would say, is the heart of the poem : the old convention of *Lycidas*, the trust in the Sicilian Muse; and the blending of the Greek pastoral mythology with the life of the English friends, in their great country house.